Brick Science

STEM Tips and Tricks for Experimenting with Your LEGO® Bricks

Jacquie Fisher, M.S.

Sky Pony Press
New York

Table of Contents

An Introduction to Brick Science

Welcome to Brick Science! The projects and activities in this book will inspire kids to explore different areas of science as they create, experiment, and build with bricks.

Tips for Using this Book (A Note for Parents & Educators)

Kids will be introduced to science concepts in the areas of biology, physics, chemistry, Earth science, astronomy, and more while they learn through play and engineering along with trial and error. Most of the projects and activities are what we call an "open build concept," meaning that kids can put their own twist on how they will create and build their models and experiments. If specific items or ingredients are required, the details will be listed in the "Supplies" area for that activity. Each project also includes a "Be a Scientist: Explore More!" area to encourage kids to dive deeper into the science concepts.

Each activity includes a science vocabulary list to introduce children to scientific terms. Most projects can be done either inside or outdoors, but a few do require outdoor-only environments to test the project (such as the brick sundial and rain gauge)

The Resource section will help identify which projects are considered beginner, intermediate, and advanced regarding the science concepts incorporated into the activity. Typically, beginner projects are used with preschool through 2nd grade, Intermediate projects with 3rd–5th grade and Advanced projects with middle school ages. However, if your child has an interest in a project, do let them try it! Desire to try a project should always outweigh the age recommendations.

For Kids

Are you ready to try some cool science activities, create some amazing experiments, and use bricks in a whole new way?

From this point forward, you are officially a Brick Scientist!

Each of the experiments, models, and projects in this book will explore different areas of science—biology, chemistry, physics, Earth science, astronomy, and more. As with any area of science, there are always a few principles that should be followed—standards that will be used as we complete the various science activities.

Meet the Brick Scientists

Let's meet the three Brick Scientists who will introduce us to the standards and principles we will follow during the awesome experiments and projects in this book!

MEET ATOM

Favorite Scientist:
Albert Einstein, physicist
Favorite Science Tool:
A magnifying glass
Frequently Says:
"Safety first!"

Atom likes to play by the rules and follow directions. He knows that even small mistakes during a science project can mean danger! If you see Atom during one of the experiments, it means you should always wear your safety gear, follow the directions, and be sure to take precautions to keep yourself and others safe.

MEET ADA

Favorite Scientist:

Marie Curie, chemist

Favorite Science Tool:

A notebook – many scientists use notebooks to write and draw their experiments and findings.

Frequently Says:

"Pay attention to the details"

Ada loves taking notes during her experiments and projects! She also draws pictures of her experiments and uses her computer to keep track of data she collects during her project. When Ada's around, it means the project has specific instructions that should be followed, kind of like a recipe. If you skip one of the steps or do them out of order, the experiment may not work!

MEET CHARLIE

Favorite Scientist:

Charles Darwin, naturalist

Favorite Science Tool:

Safety goggles

Frequently Says:

"Will this work the right way?"

Charlie knows that some science experiments and activities can involve many steps and use ingredients that are new or unfamiliar. In science, it's important to remember that we need to read carefully, ask questions if we are unsure, and know that the outcome might be different than we expected—and that's ok!

Exploring Earth Science with Bricks

Earth science is the branch of science that focuses on the Earth and its atmosphere. It includes the areas of geology, the weather, the oceans, biomes, and environmental issues.

We will explore Earth science using bricks for the following activities and projects:

- Building a Dinosaur Dig to learn about fossils and paleontology.
- Creating a model of the layers of the atmosphere.
- Learning about water and the environment by making a Brick Water Cycle model.
- Using items from nature to create data graphs and tables.
- Exploring how ancient people tracked time using the sun with a Brick Sundial.
- Measuring the weather by constructing a rain gauge.
- Investigating the night sky by building constellations.

DIY BRICK DINOSAUR DIG

Wouldn't it be cool to discover a dinosaur bone or fossil?

Or even a whole dinosaur skeleton?

Scientists who dig up and study the fossils of plants and prehistoric animals are called paleontologists. While it is hard to go out and find real dinosaur bones or fossils, you can learn how to be a paleontologist at home by building your own Brick Dinosaur Dig! *(If you are an adult reading this book, this is also a cool activity for a birthday party or summer camp!)*

BUILDING A DINOSAUR SKELETON

For this science activity, you'll need the following supplies:

- A large baseplate
- White or light gray bricks in the following sizes: 1x2, 1x3, 1x4, and 1x6
- Some sand which will be used to cover your fossil
- A medium sized paint brush
- A shallow plastic tub or sandbox large enough to hold the baseplate
- Safety goggles

SCIENCE VOCABULARY

PALEONTOLOGY: the study of plant fossils and animal fossils

FOSSIL: any remains or impression of a prehistoric animal or plant that once lived on Earth

SEDIMENTARY ROCK: rocks formed in layers and made of sand, mud, pebbles, and other materials that are pushed together and harden over time

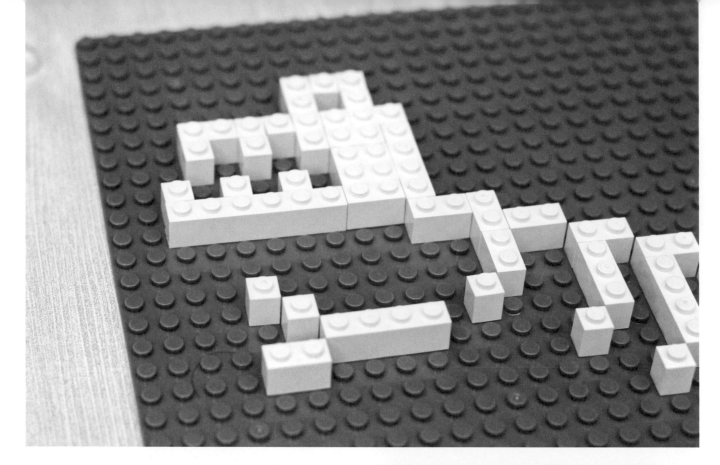

We modeled our dinosaur after a Tyrannosaurus Rex. The skeleton has a longer body with shorter arms and legs. This is an open build, so your dinosaur skeleton does not have to look exactly like ours; feel free to create your favorite type of dinosaur!

To build the dinosaur skeleton, we used white bricks to represent the bones of the dinosaur. Construct the dinosaur's skeleton from a side view—think of it as though he was lying down to take a nap!

First, make a small square with an opening in the center to represent the eye socket in the dinosaur's skull. Then use bricks to build up part of the jaw and mouth, adding in a few 1x1 bricks for teeth. Remember, when any fossil is found, it is usually missing some of the bones. Do not be overly concerned with making a complete skeleton—all the bones do not have to connect.

Once we completed the dinosaur's head, we used 1x2 bricks to shape a backbone and then extended 1x3 and 1x4 bricks from the backbone to create some ribs.

We then used some larger bricks for the body area to represent the hips and added some 1x4 and 1x2 bricks to create two legs, feet, and an arm. Last, we extended shorter bricks (1x2 and 1x1) off the end of the body to add a small tail.

Be creative with this build! There is no right or wrong way to make a dinosaur skeleton.

Here is what our final dinosaur skeleton looks like before he is covered in sand. Feel free to copy this example or go off and create your own!

SETTING UP THE DINOSAUR DIG

Fossils are usually found in rocks that form when sand, mud, and other materials settle and create layers. This type of layered rock is called sedimentary rock.

To set up a Dinosaur Dig, we are going to need to cover our skeleton with some layers! We chose to use sand to cover our dinosaur, however you can also use dry dirt if sand is not available. Be sure that it is easy to brush away the sand or dirt with a dry paintbrush so you can uncover your fossil during the dig.

Once you finish building your dinosaur skeleton, place the baseplate into a shallow plastic container or a sandbox. Next, carefully pour sand over the top of your fossil and baseplate. You may want to wear your safety goggles to protect your eyes when pouring the sand over your skeleton.

Be sure to cover the whole baseplate and all the bricks entirely so you are not able to see any of your dinosaur's skeleton! Just do not put on too much sand or it will take a long time to brush off as you dig out your fossil.

Once the skeleton is covered, use a paint brush to carefully brush away sand from various places until you can see the top of some of your fossil (the white bricks). When a paleontologist first sees part of a fossil, it is called a fragment. Once you have found a fragment, carefully continue to brush away the layers of sand to help reveal more of the dinosaur until you have uncovered the entire fossil!

BE A SCIENTIST: EXPLORE MORE!

Many times, paleontologists use special materials to create a mold or impression of the fossil before moving it. These impressions are called casts.

You can also use your brick skeleton to create a cast or mold of the fossil using clay or playdough. After you have created your brick skeleton, cover the bricks with a thin layer of playdough or clay. Then carefully peel off the playdough or clay to reveal a cast of your fossil!

LEARNING THE LAYERS OF THE ATMOSPHERE

When you look up in the sky, you will see a lot of blue and maybe some white clouds. If you are lucky, you might see an airplane or birds flying overhead too!

Did you know that the sky has layers just like a cake?

All the air and gases that surround the Earth are called its atmosphere. Clouds are formed in one layer of the atmosphere, temperatures can be very hot or very cold in different layers of the atmosphere, and depending on which type of plane you see, they fly in various layers too.

For this project, we are going to build a model of the Earth's atmosphere and learn more about what happens as we get closer to outer space!

CREATING A MODEL OF THE EARTH'S ATMOSPHERE

To build this model, you will need the following types of bricks:

- A baseplate
- Five different colors of bricks (you will need quite a few of each color!)
- Yellow bricks (for the ozone layer)
- Optional items: white bricks (to use for clouds); a brick rocket or plane if you have one

SCIENCE VOCABULARY

ATMOSPHERE: the layers of gases (also called air) that surround a planet; the Earth's atmosphere includes five distinct layers

METEOROLOGIST: a weather forecaster; someone who studies the weather in the atmosphere

TROPOSPHERE: first layer of the atmosphere located closest to the Earth

STRATOSPHERE: second layer of the Earth's atmosphere, includes the ozone layer

MESOSPHERE: third layer of the Earth's atmosphere

THERMOSPHERE: fourth and hottest layer of the Earth's atmosphere

EXOSPHERE: the top and coldest layer of the Earth's atmosphere

To create a model of the Earth's atmosphere, you will be building a brick wall with different color layers on your baseplate. We chose to use various shades of green, blue, gray, and black for our atmospheric layers. You can choose any color bricks you would like for each of five layers but be sure to use a *different* color for each layer of the atmosphere.

The Troposphere

The first layer of the atmosphere is called the troposphere. This layer includes the air we breathe and begins at the ground continuing up eight to fourteen kilometers (approximately five to nine miles) above the Earth's surface. We used green bricks to build our troposphere along with a few white bricks to represent clouds.

A lot of activity happens in the troposphere:

- People, animals, plants, and trees live here.
- Almost all the weather (fog, clouds, rain, and lightning) occurs in this level.
- Hot air balloons and small planes fly in this layer of the atmosphere.
- The air in this part of the atmosphere is the densest.

The Stratosphere

The next layer of the atmosphere is the stratosphere. This area of the atmosphere also includes another important section—the ozone layer. The stratosphere starts just above the troposphere and extends to 50 kilometers (31 miles) high. The ozone layer, which absorbs and scatters

the sun's ultraviolet radiation, is located at 20 kilometers. We used blue bricks to represent the stratosphere and yellow bricks for the ozone layer.

There is still quite a bit of activity in the stratosphere:

- Larger passenger planes and jets fly in this layer BELOW the ozone layer.
- Military jet planes can fly in this layer both above and below the ozone layer.
- Meteorologists can send weather balloons up to this layer to measure the atmosphere.
- The air in this layer is very dry so there are NO clouds, rain, or snow.

The Mesosphere

The third layer of the atmosphere is called the mesosphere. Now we are quite far above the Earth's surface. This layer extends from 50 kilometers (at the top the stratosphere) up to 85 kilometers (or 53 miles high). We used a thinner layer of light gray bricks to create our mesosphere.

It is COLD in this layer of the atmosphere! Temperatures can reach a chilly -90° C (-130° F)! Meteorites (also known as shooting stars) burn up in this layer too. This layer of the atmosphere is very hard to study so scientists know very little about what happens in the mesosphere.

The Thermosphere

The air in the thermosphere is very thin. This layer begins just above the mesosphere and continues up 600 kilometers (or 372 miles) high. The thermosphere in our model was constructed using dark gray bricks.

This is the hottest layer of the Earth's atmosphere; temperatures can reach 4500°F! Satellites orbit the Earth in this layer. Auroras (such as the Northern Lights and Southern Lights) also occur in this layer.

The Exosphere

The exosphere is the top layer of the Earth's atmosphere. It extends up to 10,000 kilometers (6,200 miles). This is where our atmosphere meets outer space! We used black bricks to create this layer of our atmosphere.

The air is very thin in this layer and it is extremely cold. GPS satellites orbit the Earth in this layer (near 20,000 kilometers high).

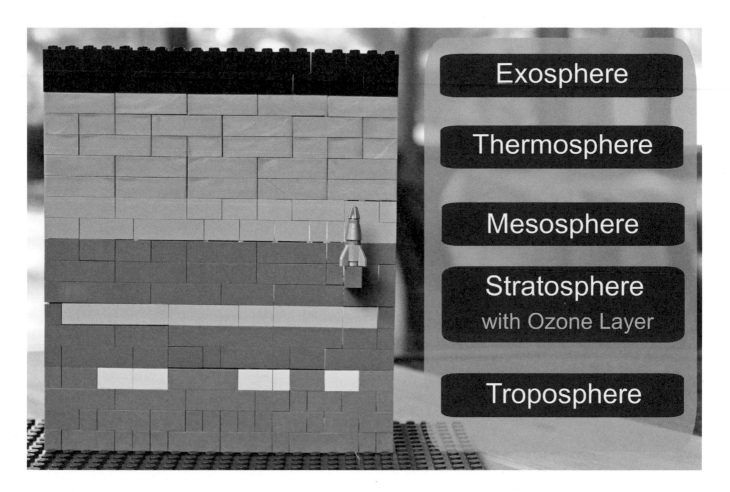

Exosphere

Thermosphere

Mesosphere

Stratosphere
with Ozone Layer

Troposphere

Here is what our final model of the Earth's atmosphere looks like once completed. We included labels for each of the atmospheric layers.

BE A SCIENTIST: EXPLORE MORE!

The Earth itself also has layers! There are four layers of the Earth: the crust, the mantle, the outer core, and the inner core. Research each of these four layers and use different color bricks to create your own model of the Earth's layers!

CREATING A MODEL OF THE WATER CYCLE

Did you know that the water that exists on Earth has been here for millions of years? The water we drink today is the same water that dinosaurs drank!

Water does not leave the Earth's atmosphere; it just changes forms during a process we call the water cycle. For this activity, we are going to build a Brick Water Cycle model and learn how water travels through its different forms.

BUILDING A BRICK WATER CYCLE

For your Brick Water Cycle, you will need the following items:

- A baseplate – choose a neutral color such as white, gray, tan, or clear
- Ten to twenty white bricks of various sizes
- Ten gray bricks sizes 1x1 and 1x2
- Ten to twenty yellow bricks of various sizes
- Ten to twenty blue bricks of various sizes
- Ten to twenty green or brown bricks

SCIENCE VOCABULARY

PRECIPITATION: a weather condition where some type of moisture (such as rain, snow, sleet, or hail) falls from the sky

EVAPORATION: the process of something turning from a liquid to a vapor

CONDENSATION: the process by which water vapor is changed into a liquid

Water is a finite resource on Earth. The water cycle includes three main parts: precipitation, evaporation, and condensation.

Water molecules that exist in lakes, rivers, and oceans travel through the water cycle. These molecules move from those bodies of water into the air around us as water vapor. The water vapor then forms into clouds. Clouds create rain, sleet, or snow, and the water is returned to the Earth again.

Precipitation

Precipitation occurs when some type of moisture falls from the sky. For the first part of our model, we need to build a cloud. Use your white bricks to create a cloud on the top-left side of your baseplate. Then use your gray bricks to add some precipitation—rain, sleet, or snow—under the cloud.

Next, build a green or brown area representing land on the bottom-left side of your baseplate under the cloud. You could also add some trees if you would like to! This is the first part of the water cycle which shows precipitation falling from a cloud down to the Earth.

Evaporation

For the next part of the water cycle, use blue bricks to build an area of water on the bottom-right side of the baseplate (to the right of your land area). The blue area represents the lakes, rivers, and oceans on Earth.

Now use the yellow bricks to create the sun in the upper, right corner of the base-plate over your water. Then place some smaller blue bricks above your large area of water and below the Sun. These small blue bricks show us that evaporation happens when heat from the sun radiates over bodies of water. As the water warms, some of the water molecules turn into water vapor which rises into the air.

Condensation

The third part of the cycle is condensation. This is what happens when water vapor in

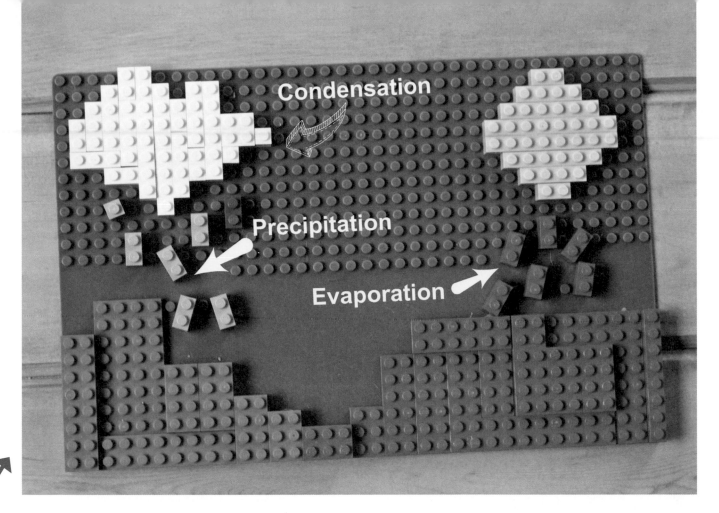

the air is transformed into clouds. Clouds are collections of water vapor and particles. The cloud that was built during the first part of our project shows us that condensation occurs during the water cycle. When finished, your Brick Water Cycle should look like the photo above.

HOW DOES THE WATER CYCLE WORK?

Clouds produce different types of precipitation such as rain, sleet, and snow. The precipitation falls to Earth and drains into our lakes, rivers, and oceans. As the sun heats the atmosphere, droplets from those bodies of water begin to evaporate into the air (or the first layer of the atmosphere as we learned with our last project!). Once the droplets reach the upper layer of the tro-

posphere, they condense and form clouds. And the cycle begins all over again. This explains why we drink the same water as dinosaurs did years ago—water just recycles itself over and over!

BE A SCIENTIST: EXPLORE MORE!

Transpiration is another activity that occurs during the water cycle. Transpiration is the evaporation of water from a plant or tree's leaves into the air. Build a plant or tree on the land section of your water cycle model to show how transpiration occurs!

MAKING 2D AND 3D BAR GRAPHS

All scientists LOVE data!

Data is a fancy word for information, facts, or statistics that are collected so they can easily be analyzed or looked at again in the future. By collecting data, scientists can keep track of the information gathered during their experiment and use it to determine if the experiment worked the way they predicted. A graph is a fun way to organize data so you can quickly refer to the information to answer questions.

Here is one example of why you would want to collect and graph data:

Let's say you went on a nature walk and collected leaves, pinecones, acorns, and tree seeds. You might come home with a big pile of nature items!

When you tell your friends about all the cool things you found, they might ask you questions like—

"Did you find more pinecones or acorns?" or *"Were there more red leaves or yellow leaves?"*

By sorting and graphing your data, you will quickly be able to answer their questions!

SCIENCE VOCABULARY

DATA: facts, information, and statistics collected for analysis and reference

GRAPH: a visual diagram or layout showing the relationship among two or more items

CREATING BAR GRAPHS

Here is what you will need for this science activity:

- One baseplate
- Black bricks sizes 1x2, 1x3 or 1x4 (or a combination of these sizes)
- Various color bricks size 2x2—you will need one color brick for each type of item you collect
- A collection of nature items—you can use different color leaves, or other nature items such as green leaves, rocks, pinecones, and acorns

Once you collect your data, it is important to organize it so you can quickly make comparisons. For this project, we are going to make two types of bar graphs to display the items (data) that were collected.

2-DIMENSIONAL (2D) BAR GRAPHS

A 2-dimensional (or 2D) bar graph lays flat on your baseplate so all the bars on your graph are only one brick high.

Using black bricks, create an L shape near the outer left and bottom edges of your baseplate. This will be used as the frame of your graph. The line across the bottom of your baseplate is called the horizontal axis, and the line on the left side of your baseplate is the vertical axis.

For our project, we collected a variety of colored leaves. We used one color brick to represent each leaf color: yellow bricks for the yellow leaves, blue bricks

Only use leaves that are found on the ground!

If there's a leaf on a tree, please 'leaf' it alone

for the green leaves, gray bricks for the silver leaves, etc. Your bricks do not have to be the same color as your leaves. For example, we used blue bricks to represent our dark green leaves since the color of our baseplate is already green. If you do not have colored leaves available for this activity, use green leaves and graph them

based on their shape. Or collect tree seeds such as acorns, pinecones, tree pods, and nuts to graph.

To build the graph, use one 2x2 brick for each leaf in the color group. Beginning on the horizontal axis (the black bricks at the bottom of the baseplate) of the graph, place bricks beside one another building towards the top of the baseplate. Based on the number of bricks used for each leaf color, you can see that on our nature walk, we found:

- five yellow leaves
- three dark green leaves
- two silver leaves
- six red leaves and
- four light green leaves

You can quickly see that we found more red leaves than any other color just by viewing the height of the brick bars that were built on the graph! The graph also shows that the silver leaves were the smallest number collected on our walk.

3-DIMENSIONAL BAR GRAPHS

A three-dimensional (or 3D) bar graph can be created by stacking your bricks on top of each other in one tall tower instead of laying each of them on the baseplate.

We used the same number and color of leaves for the 3D bar graph as we did for the flat (2-dimensional) bar graph. Again, you can quickly see that the tallest tower of bricks is red, which tells us that the largest number of leaves in our collection were red. The 3D bars also make it easy to see that the silver leaves were the smallest number collected.

BE A SCIENTIST: EXPLORE MORE!

Go outside and collect a variety of nature items—acorns, pinecones, rocks, sticks, and leaves. Assign a brick color to each item. Then build a 2D or 3D bar graph using your nature "data"!

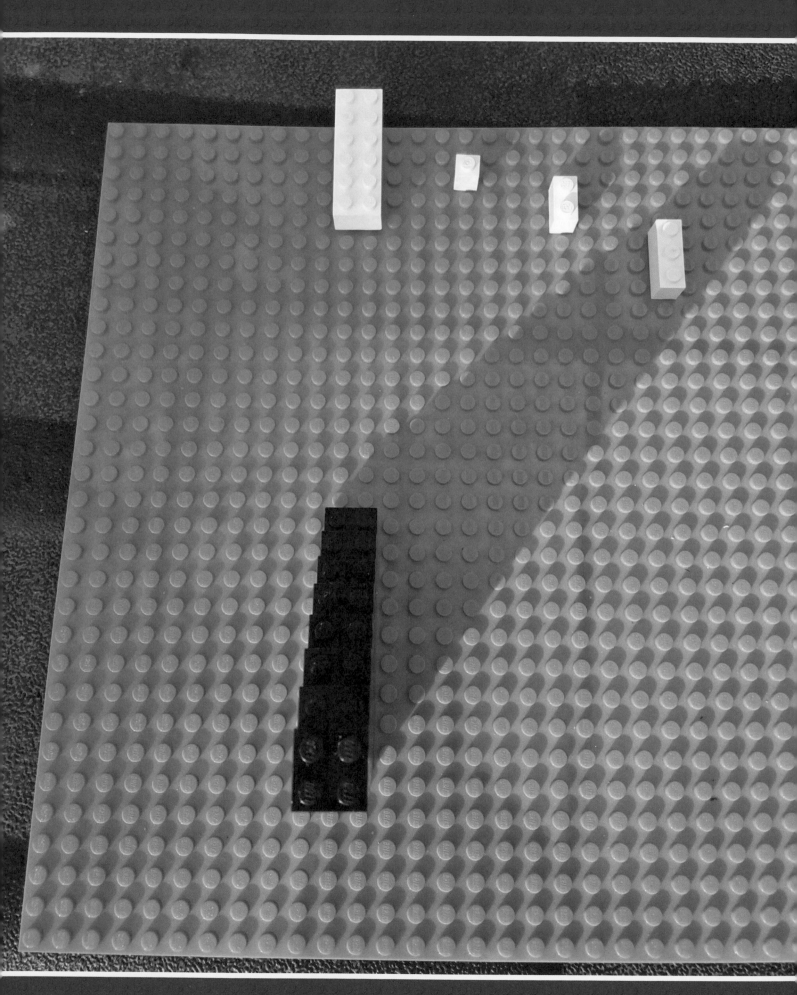

TELLING TIME WITH A BRICK SUNDIAL

Sundials were used in ancient societies to measure the time of day. They are some of the oldest scientific instruments in the world! A sundial tells us the time of day like a clock, only it uses light from the sun to cast a shadow on markings that represent each hour of the day.

Please note: This project is NOT meant to be an accurate timekeeper—although you will be able to use it to tell the approximate time of day. Instead, the goal of this activity is to show how ancient civilizations tracked time before the invention of modern-day clocks.

BUILDING A BRICK SUNDIAL

You will need the following supplies to create your sundial:

- A light color baseplate (we chose to use orange—white and yellow are also good options)
- Black bricks to use for your gnomon
- Light color bricks to mark the hours of the day (make sure they are a different color than your baseplate!)
- A clock or watch
- A compass or knowledge of cardinal directions
- An open space outside where you can place the sundial
- A sunny day (this activity will ONLY work outdoors using the sun)

SCIENCE VOCABULARY

SUNDIAL: an instrument that shows the time of day using the shadow cast by the gnomon or pointer onto a plate marked with the hours of the day

GNOMON: the piece of a sundial that casts a shadow to show the time, sometimes referred to as the pointer

Constructing the Gnomon

The first step to creating a sundial is to build the gnomon. You will want to build your gnomon high enough that it will cast a shadow across your baseplate.

We built our gnomon eight bricks high while each of our time markers is only one brick high. We also chose to have an angled gnomon instead of using a single stack of bricks. An angled gnomon will allow you to move the sundial to different locations and still get an accurate reading. To construct an angled gnomon, use your bricks to build a small set of stairs. Beginning at the bottom-center of your baseplate, lay down a line of bricks that are about seven to nine studs long.

The bottom row should be your longest row; ours was nine studs long. A stud is one of the small knobs located on the top of your bricks. The top row of the gnomon will be the shortest row (ours was two studs long). As we stacked our bricks, we decreased each row by one stud to create the staircase look.

Positioning the Sundial and Marking the Hours

A sundial is built with markings for daytime hours only. Since a sundial relies on sunlight, it will not tell time during hours that occur in the evening (at or after dusk) or throughout the night since there is no source of sunlight available.

A sundial needs to point north and sit on a flat surface to show the correct time of day. As the sun shines on the sundial, the gnomon will cast a shadow. Place your sundial outside, on a flat surface with the gnomon pointing north. Use a compass to find north if you are unsure of your location.

When the sun is at its highest point (approximately 12:00 noon), it will cast a short shadow. As the sun sits lower in the sky (both at dusk and dawn), longer shadows will be created on the sundial. Use a watch to determine when it is 12:00 p.m. (also referred to as 12:00 noon). At that time, add a white brick near the end of the shadow that is cast on the sundial. When a shadow falls on this brick, you will know that it is approximately 12:00 noon.

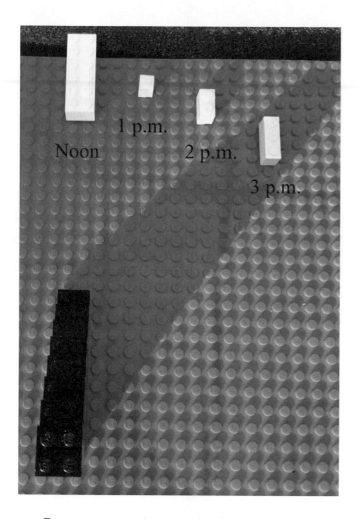

Noon   1 p.m.   2 p.m.   3 p.m.

Repeat every hour, placing a new white brick near the end of the shadow cast at 1 p.m., 2 p.m., 3 p.m., etc. for as long as the gnomon continues to cast a shadow on the baseplate. To mark the morning hours, leave the sundial in the same spot overnight and then add a white brick to mark each of the morning hours.

For our sundial, we coordinated the number of studs on our bricks with the hour of day when marking the time. For example, the brick marking 12 noon has twelve studs and the brick marking the 1 p.m. hour has one stud.

Once your sundial has white bricks marking the hours, you will be able to use it to tell the approximate time of day. Please be aware that the length of the shadow will change over time depending on where you live, the time of the year, and the location of the sundial. For example, as the Earth tilts towards or away from the sun during different seasons, the light from the position of the sun over your sundial will also change.

A side note: Your sundial will NOT look like a clock face where the time markings are evenly spaced over 12 hours. The markings on a sundial will be closer together since you will most likely have more than twelve markings once you complete your project.

BE A SCIENTIST: EXPLORE MORE!

Test how accurate your sundial is at telling time! Move it to a different location, being sure to keep the gnomon pointing north. Then compare the shadows cast each hour to the time on a clock. Are the shadows still falling close to the brick markings for each hour?

BUILDING A RAIN GAUGE TO MEASURE RAINFALL

All plants and trees need water to live. Most of the water they use comes from rainfall. But how do we know if enough rain has fallen to keep the plants and trees healthy? One way to measure rainfall is by using a rain gauge. A rain gauge is a weather instrument that helps to measure the amount of rain that falls during a specific time period.

BUILDING A RAIN GAUGE

To construct a rain gauge, you will need the following items:

- A baseplate
- A ruler—one that can be left outdoors and get wet
- A small, empty plastic water bottle
- Blue bricks sizes 2x2, 3x2, and 1x4 to use for the base holders
- Yellow bricks sizes 1x2 or 1x3 to stabilize the water bottle

SCIENCE VOCABULARY

RAINFALL: the amount of rain that falls in a certain area within a specific amount of time

GAUGE: an instrument that measures the amount of some object, such as rain

First, place the empty water bottle on your baseplate. Then use blue bricks to build a square frame around the bottom of the water bottle. Be sure there are bricks on all four corners surrounding the bottle so it will not tip over in the wind or rain.

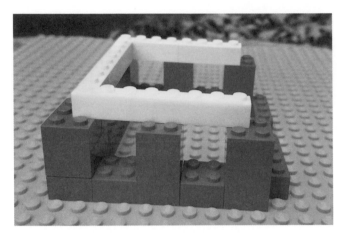

It is important to leave some open areas in your frame. As you can see in the photo, the second and third layers of bricks were alternated in high and low positions so that it is possible to view water collected in the bottom of the bottle when it rains.

Once the blue base is built, add yellow bricks to the inside top row of studs to hold the water bottle securely in place.

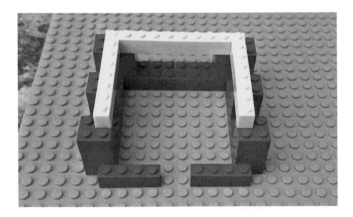

Here is our base from the top view. We only used one level of blue bricks on

the front of our base to secure the bottle. The yellow bricks will add an extra level of stability.

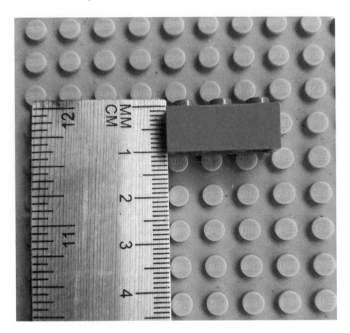

Measure the height of your bricks. The bricks we used for our project were one centimeter tall. Knowing the height of your bricks will make it easy to calculate how much rain has been collected in your water bottle.

Next to the base, build a thin stand to hold the ruler. Stack four 1x4 blue bricks to

make the back of the holder. On the front, place a 2x4 blue brick and two 1x3 bricks to use as a bottom layer for the ruler's stand.

Place the ruler with the centimeter side down into your rain gauge holder. Then place your water bottle into its stand. Wiggle your baseplate side to side a little to be sure both items feel secure. If needed, add another level of bricks to secure either item.

Position your rain gauge outside on a flat surface in an open area (not too close to any building, trees, or shrubs). Now watch your weather forecast so you know when rain is expected! After receiving some rain, check your rain gauge to see how much precipitation was collected. Use the ruler to measure the amount of rainfall you received.

BE A SCIENTIST: EXPLORE MORE!

Compare your rainfall collection with the official collection numbers! Visit an online weather website (such as your local news station or weather.com) to learn how much rain fell in your area. How close were your measurements to the actual rainfall amounts?

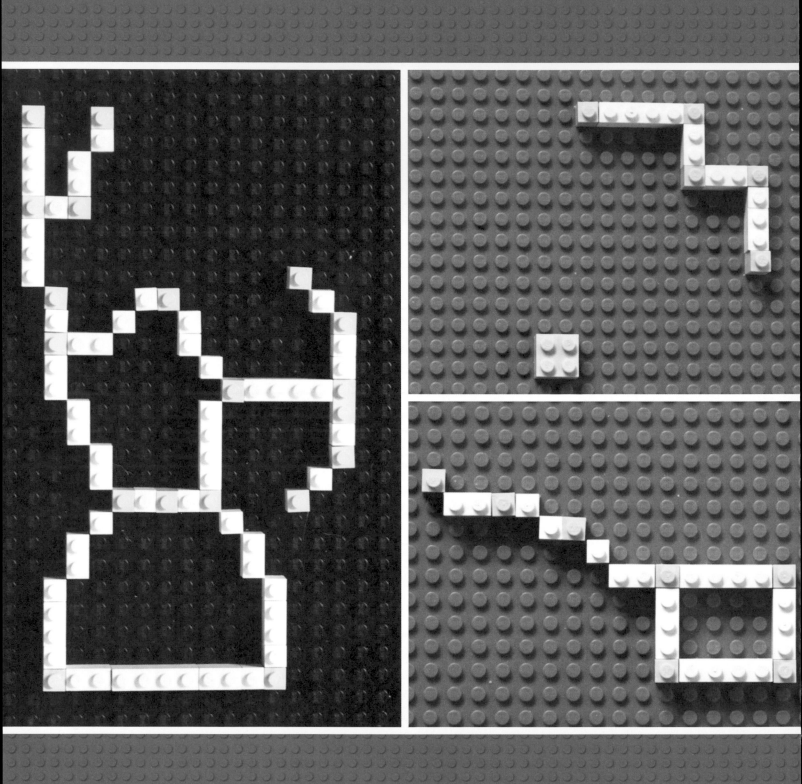

BUILDING CONSTELLATIONS

Constellations are clusters of stars that form an imaginary image when viewed from Earth. Our nighttime sky is divided into 88 constellations that can be viewed from locations around the globe. These star patterns are highlighted on star maps. Many constellation patterns resemble animals, mythical creatures, and objects such as a compass or crown.

For this project, we will build three of the most well-known constellations: Orion, the Big Dipper (part of the Ursa Major constellation), and Cassiopeia.

CREATING CONSTELLATIONS

For this science activity, you will need the following items:

- **A large, dark colored baseplate**
- **White bricks sizes 1x1, 1x2, 1x3, and 1x4**
- **A variety of 1x1 yellow bricks**
- **One 2x2 yellow brick**

To build each brick constellation, use yellow bricks to represent the main stars in that constellation and white bricks to represent the imaginary lines that help to outline the constellation's shape.

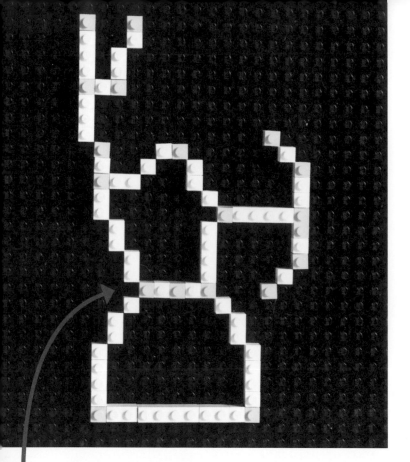

Orion, the Hunter

Orion is named after a hunter from Greek mythology and is one of the brightest constellations in the winter sky. Its location allows it to be viewed from places around the world. Orion includes two bright stars, Betelgeuse and Rigel.

To build Orion, begin with three yellow bricks for his belt, adding one white brick between each yellow one. Next, add a yellow brick for each star of his two feet. Use white bricks to connect his belt to his feet and more white bricks to create the imaginary line between the two feet.

For the upper part of the constellation, follow the photo above as a guide for your yellow and white bricks, building up from Orion's belt. Legends tell us that Orion is holding a club in his right hand and a lion's pelt in his left hand.

Polaris, the Big Dipper, and Cassiopeia

We are constructing these two constellations together since the locations of both are related to Polaris (the North Star) in the night sky. Place a 2x2 yellow brick in the center of your baseplate—this will represent the North Star.

The Big Dipper is part of the Ursa Major constellation. Two of the stars in this constellation point to Polaris, the North Star. The Big Dipper is shaped like a pot with a handle. Use yellow bricks for each of the four corners of the pot, connecting them with white bricks. Then build the handle, being sure to include the three yellow bricks (which represent the constellation's stars) as you build.

Cassiopeia is named after a mythical queen from ancient Greece. The constellation has a "W" shape and resembles a crown, which makes it 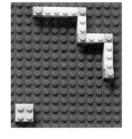 easy to find in the night sky. The middle star of Cassiopeia points to the North Star, so place that brick on your baseplate first. Then use the photo as a guide to finish creating the constellation.

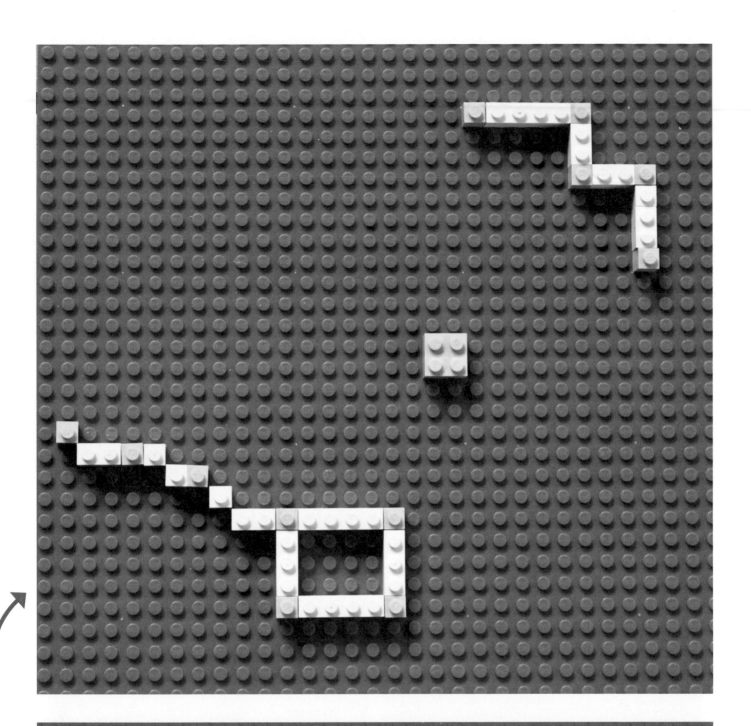

BE A SCIENTIST: EXPLORE MORE!

Visit https://staratlas.com to see all the constellations that exist in the night sky. Choose a different constellation to build with your bricks!

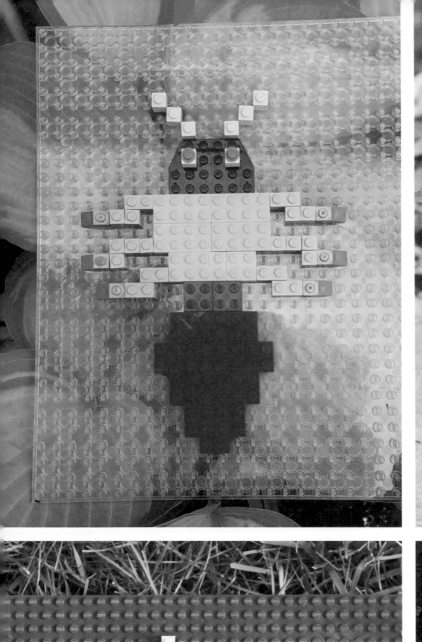

Brick Biology

Biology is the study of all living things.

The science of biology covers many areas such as the human body and cells, the study of plants (called botany), how living things interact with their environment (the science of ecology), and the study of animals (referred to as zoology).

For this area of science, we will use bricks for the following projects:

- Learning the parts of an insect by inventing your own Brick Bug.
- Constructing a Brick Bug House to attract insects.
- Observing how worms live with a Brick Worm Viewer.
- Engineering a Brick Exoskeleton to understand how it protects animals and insects.
- Building a Brick Leaf model to explore the parts of a leaf and learn how they function.
- Taking an inside look at a leaf by constructing a Brick Plant Cell.
- Creating a Brick Model of the Human Tongue to learn about the science of taste.

CREATING YOUR OWN BRICK INSECT

Have you ever wondered how to identify an insect? Scientists who study insects are called entomologists.

You and I may refer to many of these small creatures as "bugs," but they are called insects in the science world! For this project, we will build our own Brick Bug by learning the main body parts ALL insects must have in order to be labeled an "insect".

BUILDING A BRICK INSECT

Gather the following supplies for this project:

- A large baseplate
- A variety of bricks in six different colors
- Some creative thinking since you will be making your own bug!

SCIENCE VOCABULARY

THORAX: the middle body part of an insect, located between its head and abdomen

ANTENNAE: long, thin body parts of an insect that grow off its head

COMPOUND EYE: an eye consisting of multiple visual units

ENTOMOLOGIST: a person or scientist who studies insects

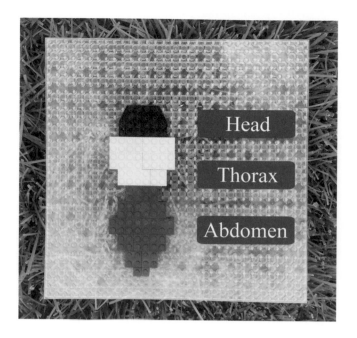

While there are many different types of insects in the world, such as bees, butterflies, and grasshoppers, all insects have three main body parts:

- a head,
- a thorax, and
- an abdomen

Insects also have three pairs of legs (six legs in total), a set of eyes, and one pair of antennae.

To build your bug, choose one color of bricks for its head, a second color for its thorax, and a third color for its abdomen.

We used the following colors of bricks for our insect:

- black bricks for the head,
- yellow bricks for the thorax, and
- red bricks for the insect's abdomen

The insect's head is usually the smallest part of its body while the abdomen is the largest body section.

For most insects, the head includes a set of compound eyes along with a mouth. We used white and orange bricks to create our eyes. We decided the mouth of our insect would be located on the underside of the head and not able to be seen from the top view.

The head is also the location for a pair of antennae; add two antennae on your insect's head. The antennae act as sensory organs and help the insect to smell, taste, touch, and even hear (it is like having a tongue, ears, nose, and fingers all in one organ!).

The thorax (the middle body section of an insect) is where the legs are located. Remember, all insects have three sets of legs so be sure your bug has six legs. And an insect's legs have joints—an area of the leg that can bend—just like our knee joint. We created our legs using gray bricks and built them at an angle to show they are jointed.

If an insect has wings, these are also located on the midsection of their body. If your insect will have wings, attach those to the top of its thorax, above the legs.

There it is—a complete insect with all its necessary body parts!

BE A SCIENTIST: EXPLORE MORE!

What do insects do? Some insects fly while others crawl. Some live under ground and others live in trees. Make a list of the characteristics of your bug. Where does it live? How does it eat? How does it move around?

CONSTRUCTING A BUG HOTEL

If you walk outside and look under a rock or near a tree, you will find a few crawling or flying bugs. Bugs are also known as insects, and there are more than 900,000 different kinds that live on Earth!

Did you ever wonder what insects do all day? For this project, we are going to build a Bug Hotel out of bricks so we can observe what insects do during the day.

Insects that visit your "bug hotel" may decide to build a nest, hibernate, or store their food there! And by inviting more insects into your yard, you will increase the biodiversity of the area and encourage flowers and plants to grow!

BUILDING YOUR BUG HOTEL

First, we will use bricks to create a cube or box that is open on four sides but has walls on the other two sides. You will need the following supplies for your Bug Hotel:

- 100-200 bricks in colors you would normally see in an outdoor area (blue, green, brown, tan, yellow, red, and black)
- Cardboard tubes (for example, the cardboard that comes in paper towel rolls)
- Lint from a clothes dryer or cotton balls
- A handful of twigs and sticks
- Some large leaves

SCIENCE VOCABULARY

BIODIVERSITY: the variety of life in a specific habitat
HABITAT: the natural home or environment of an animal, plant, or insect
POLLINATOR: an animal or insect that moves pollen from one plant to another. This helps the plants and flowers to produce fruits or seeds.
CAMOUFLAGE: to hide an object by surrounding it with colors or items normally found in the area

Begin by building two large brick squares with open centers to use for the top and bottom of the bug house. You can see in the photo that our squares are blue and are two bricks tall.

Next, build walls on two sides of the bottom square. We used yellow, green, and blue bricks to build our side walls.

Then attach the second open square to the top of those walls. Your bug house can be square or rectangular, tall or short!

The next step is to add the cardboard tubes into the open space in your Bug Hotel. This will help hold the other materials in place.

Once your cardboard tubes are in place, fill them with twigs, sticks, and some of the dryer lint or cotton balls so that insects will have places to crawl and hide when they visit your bug hotel.

BE A SCIENTIST: EXPLORE MORE!

Who is visiting your hotel?

Place your bug hotel in a garden or outdoor area that includes plants and trees. Once it has been in place for a few days, peek to see if any insects are visiting. Do not lift or move the brick hotel—instead, carefully remove a few of the leaves or sticks. Make a list of the types of insects that visit your hotel over the next few weeks.

Last, use the leaves to cover the top of your Bug Hotel. The leaves offer some camouflage so the brick building will blend in with the rest of your yard or outdoor area.

BRICK WORM VIEWER AND HABITAT

This brick science project will give us an inside look at the life of a worm!

Earthworms are cold-blooded animals. They do not have any arms, legs, or eyes, but they perform a very important job! Earthworms spend most of their lives underground digging their way through soil and dirt. As they dig, worms help to increase the amount of water and air in the soil. And worms also help to break down leaves and grass into items used by plants and trees.

BUILDING A WORM VIEWER

Collect the following supplies to construct the worm viewer:

- Small brick base plates: sizes 2x3, 2x4, 2x6, and 2x8
- Red, brown, black, and tan bricks—depending on the size of your viewer, you will need between seventy-five and 150 bricks
- Nine to twelve clear bricks (for example, brick windows or bricks that have no color or shading)
- Some dirt or potting soil
- Dead leaves or cut grass
- A small amount of sand
- A worm or two, but wait until the viewer is built and habitat is constructed

ASK A PARENT FOR HELP WITH THIS ACTIVITY

This activity MUST be done with an adult since it will involve a living creature. Please do not harm your worm in any way! Any worm that is placed in the worm viewer should be kept outside, in a well shaded area. Worms should only be left in the viewer for a very short time (less than two hours) and then carefully returned to the soil so they can burrow underground.

SCIENCE VOCABULARY

HABITAT: the natural home or environment of an animal or plant
COLD-BLOODED ANIMAL: an animal whose body temperature changes with the surrounding environment; the animal's body does not regulate its temperature

A worm viewer should have the following features:

- **An open top**
- **An opening at the bottom**
- **At least one side with clear bricks**

The completed worm viewer should be a tall, thin, rectangular shaped brick structure with a partial opening on the bottom and a fully open top. We recommend the viewer be at least ten bricks tall to allow room for the habitat materials.

Building the base: Begin by building the bottom of the viewer using base plate bricks to create an open rectangle that is approximately ten brick studs wide by thirty brick studs long. We used 2x3, 2x4, 2x6, and 2x8 brick plates. These bricks will be touching but not connected or overlapping. Then use a second level of brick plates to make a solid floor on one side of the rectangle. As you can see in the photo, we have a solid black floor on the left side of our viewer; the bottom right side of the viewer is open.

Building side and back walls: Once you have the base size for your viewer, begin building the back and two side walls by adding red, brown, or black bricks.

Building the front wall: To complete the front wall, use one level of red bricks on top of the black brick base and then add the clear bricks up to the top.

Complete the viewer by adding some bricks to connect the front wall to the top sides. This extra level of bricks will help stabilize the viewer before adding the habitat materials.

CREATING A WORM HABITAT

Since an earthworm is a cold-blooded animal, the worm's body temperature depends on the environment around it. It is important to create a habitat in the viewer that will help the worm stay healthy. Worms need moisture, air, food, warmth, and dark places. Sunlight is bad for worms because it dries out their skin. Earthworms will eat dead plants and cut grasses that are found in their habitat.

Be sure to place your viewer on the ground, outside in a shaded area. Putting the viewer in a garden bed or under a tree are good location choices. Once the viewer is positioned, it is time to add the soil, sand, and crushed leaves or cut grass.

First, add a little water to some of the sand so it packs down easily. Then shovel some sand into the viewer for the first layer.

Next, mix the cut grass or crushed leaves into your soil. You can also add some water to the soil to make it easier to mix things together. Then add a layer of this mixture to the habitat.

We alternated layers of sand with layers of soil until our worm habitat was full. Be sure the top layer of the habitat is soil. Once your habitat is complete, it is time to look for a worm.

FINDING & CARING FOR EARTHWORMS

Worms can be found in moist soil, usually in garden areas or where plants and tall grasses grow. Carefully dig into the ground and loosely shake the dirt to find worms. If there has been a recent rainfall, worms can also be found on sidewalks or pathways (they come out from the wet soil).

Once you find a worm, carefully lift it into your hand using your fingers or ask an adult to help you with this step. Do not squeeze the worm.

Then lay it on the top layer of dirt in the worm viewer. After the worm is in place, be sure to wash your hands with soap and water.

Once the worm is on the soil, allow it to move around and explore. Do not pick it up. Think of it as a person—how would you feel if your parents picked you up every time they wanted you to move to another location? It may take a few minutes for the worm to adapt to its new surroundings.

Worms will move around and quickly burrow into the soil and sand layers in the viewer. Keep an eye on the worm once it begins to move and follow the path it makes through the habitat.

Once you have spent some time watching the worm move around the viewer (no more than two hours), it is time to return the worm back into the ground. To do this, carefully lift the viewer and allow the dirt, sand, and worm to slowly slide out of the bottom opening. We released our habitat material into a garden area. If the worm is visible, gently cover it with dirt or a leaf to protect it from the sun.

BE A SCIENTIST: EXPLORE MORE!

Learn more about how worms behave by using the worm viewer to track the movements of your worm. What happens as the worm moves through the soil and sand layers? Does the worm move constantly? Or does it stop in some areas? Does the worm crawl in a straight or diagonal pattern?

ANIMAL ARMOR: ENGINEERING AN EXOSKELETON

Have you ever seen a picture of a knight in shining armor? Knights used armor to protect themselves when they would go off to fight. It is like the suit that Ironman wears too—a hard outer shell that covers and protects the soft areas of your body.

Many insects also have a hard outer shell called an exoskeleton that helps to protect the soft areas of their body. Using bricks, we will build an exoskeleton for a stuffed animal! This build is going to be a creative project. You can choose any favorite stuffed animal and build an exoskeleton for it!

SCIENCE VOCABULARY

EXOSKELETON: a rigid exterior covering for animals and insects that protects their body

CAMOUFLAGE: materials that make animals hard to see by disguising them as something else

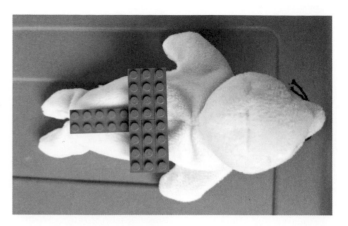

CREATING AN EXOSKELETON

Meet Sam!

Sam is a seal who lives in the ocean. He eats fish, loves to swim, and jumps through waves. But he always needs to keep an eye out for sharks! Seals and sea lions have soft bodies without anything to protect them other than a layer of thick skin. Wouldn't it be great if we could create an outer shell for a seal, like the shell on a turtle or tortoise?

Only two items are needed for this activity: a stuffed animal and a variety of bricks (at least twenty) in your favorite colors!

When building an exoskeleton, we need to consider how it's constructed so it offers protection for the animal and also allows the animal to still move, breathe, and eat. For example, Sam will need to be able to easily use his front flippers and tail to swim. And we want to let Sam move his head as much as possible too.

Since we are trying to protect Sam from sharks, our exoskeleton should cover the middle section of his body while still allowing him to be able to swim and jump in the ocean.

We started our exoskeleton by using a 2x8 green brick plate that runs from Sam's shoulders to his tail. This brick is a guide for our exterior protection since we do not want the exoskeleton to cover any of Sam's flippers.

As you build your exoskeleton, think about how your stuffed animal will need to move its arms, legs, head, and other body parts. Be sure to leave enough room around these areas so the animal can move freely while wearing the brick covering.

Next, we began adding blue bricks along the green plate that extend from the middle of Sam's back out to his sides. We decided to use blue bricks for Sam's exoskeleton since he will be swimming in the ocean and much of the water will appear blue. The blue exoskeleton will help Sam to be camouflaged in the water.

Shorter blue bricks were used closer to Sam's tail end since we wanted him

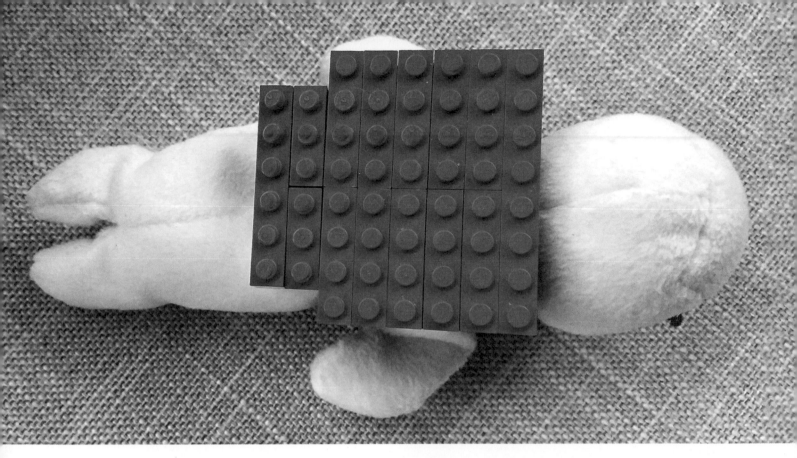

to be able to move his hind flippers both back and forth along with up and down. Remember, an exoskeleton should surround your stuffed animal's body while allowing their limbs to move freely. Once the top layer was complete, we used blue bricks to create side panels for Sam's armor. On both sides, large areas were left open for Sam's flippers.

Last, we used brick plates to connect both side panels under Sam's belly. Be sure the exoskeleton you build protects

the entire middle area of your stuffed animal—its top, bottom and all sides. Now Sam will be safer when he jumps into the ocean!

BE A SCIENTIST: EXPLORE MORE!

Take a walk in your yard or around your neighborhood and look for animals or insects that have exoskeletons. Does their exoskeleton also serve as camouflage? How does it protect the animal or insect?

EXPLORING THE PARTS OF A LEAF

Leaves play a very important role in keeping a tree alive! Leaves turn sunlight (which is solar energy) into food using the process of photosynthesis. They also provide much of the food and air a tree needs to stay alive.

Trees that have leaves (instead of needles) are called deciduous trees. For this activity, we will construct a brick model of a leaf and learn about each of its parts.

CONSTRUCTING A BRICK LEAF

Supplies that are needed for building this science model include:

- One baseplate
- A leaf to use as your model (or use the model we have in the picture)
- A large variety of bricks the same color as your leaf
- Four 1x2 green bricks
- Six 1x2 white bricks
- Twenty-eight 1x1 gray bricks

SCIENCE VOCABULARY

DECIDUOUS: a tree with leaves

PHOTOSYNTHESIS: the process plants and trees go through to make their own food using sunlight, water, and carbon dioxide

BLADE: the large, flat area of the leaf

PETIOLE: the stalk of the leaf that connects the blade to a branch

MIDRIB: the vein (or line) that runs down the center of a leaf

VEIN: small lines that run from the midrib and through the leaf's blade; veins transport water and food to the leaf and tree

First, use your leaf (or the photo above) as a model to build the main body of a brick leaf on your baseplate. Create the shape of your brick leaf to be a similar shape to the real leaf and have it cover at least half of the baseplate. This large, flat area of the leaf is called the blade. The blade is where photosynthesis occurs.

Next, use the green bricks to add a line to the bottom of your brick leaf. This is the leafstalk or petiole. The petiole is what holds the leaf on the tree.

If you look at your real leaf, you will see a line that runs down the center of the blade. Use white bricks to build a line down the center of your brick leaf—this is the leaf's midrib. The midrib provides support to the leaf—just like our spine provides us support to stand upright.

Last, use the gray bricks to build the lines you see running from the midrib. These are the leaf's veins and they carry water and nutrients throughout the leaf and back to the tree.

BE A SCIENTIST: EXPLORE MORE!

Make a leaf rubbing! Lay a leaf on a flat surface. Place a blank piece of paper over the leaf. Use the side of a crayon to rub across the entire paper—as you rub, you will see the print of a leaf appear! Identify the different parts of a leaf on your leaf print.

CONSTRUCTING A BRICK PLANT CELL

All living things are made up of cells. Cells are the smallest units of any organism and can usually only be seen with a microscope. Cells are also what keep the organism alive; they take in nutrients from food and convert them into energy.

Just like humans, plants have cells too! Plant cells include various parts each with their own job. Using bricks, we are going to build a plant cell—a super-sized version of what you would see if you looked under a microscope at a leaf or plant.

CREATING A BRICK MODEL OF A PLANT CELL

This is an advanced project and will require several types of bricks:

- A yellow baseplate
- Fifty 1x2, 1x3, and 1x4 green bricks
- Fifty 1x2, 1x3, and 1x4 blue bricks
- Ten 1x2, 1x3, and 1x4 red bricks
- Nine 1x1 gray bricks
- Nine 1x1 cream bricks
- Six 1x2 or 1x3 brown bricks
- Six 1x2 or 1x3 black bricks
- One 1x1 orange brick
- Three 2x4 green bricks
- Four purple bricks
- One 1x2 red brick
- One 2x4 red brick
- Approximately twenty white bricks

SCIENCE VOCABULARY

CELLS: the smallest unit of an organism

PHOTOSYNTHESIS: the process in which plants use sunlight, water, and carbon dioxide to create food, energy, oxygen, and water

CYTOPLASM: a jelly-like substance in a plant cell where the organelles are located

NUCLEUS: the control center of the cell; the nucleus sends instructions to the other parts of the cell to tell them how to function

VACUOLE: a storage area within the cell

ORGANELLE: a specialized structure within a cell; each organelle has a specific job it does for the cell

ROUGH ENDOPLASMIC RETICULUM (ALSO REFERRED TO AS ROUGH ER): flattened sacs in the cell's cytoplasm that help to synthesize protein

SMOOTH ENDOPLASMIC RETICULUM (ALSO CALLED SMOOTH ER): an organelle that acts as a storage area for the cell and also creates lipids (fats) and hormones

(See the next page for more vocabulary)

SCIENCE VOCABULARY

CELL WALL: a strong, protective layer that surrounds the cell membrane of plants

RIBOSOMES: a sphere-shaped structure in the cytoplasm where protein synthesis occurs

NUCLEOLUS: a small organelle that makes ribosomes

CENTROSOME: a small organelle where microtubules are made

GOLGI BODY: a flat, layered organelle located near the nucleus that prepares protein and fat molecules for use by the cell

MITOCHONDRION: finger-like organelles that produce energy for the cell

AMYLOPLAST: an organelle found in starchy plant cells (such as fruits)

CHLOROPLASTS: disc-shaped organelles that contain chlorophyll and convert sunlight into energy

CHLOROPHYLL: a green pigment found in all green plants, its job is to absorb sunlight and produce energy for the plant during the process of photosynthesis

LIPIDS: types of fats found in cells such as oils and waxes

Choose a baseplate for your plant cell. The color of your baseplate is also part of the cell called the cytoplasm. A cell's cytoplasm is a jelly-like substance where the organelles are located.

We used the following brick colors for each of our plant cell features:

Yellow baseplate = cytoplasm
Green bricks = cell wall
Blue bricks = cell membrane
Red bricks = nucleus
White bricks = vacuole

Plant cells have distinct edges, so they appear to be square or rectangular in nature. This is different from animal cells which are round. Construct a thin, green edge around the entire baseplate. This is the cell wall. The wall of the cell is thick and gives the

cell support. It also helps to bond with other cells to form the structure of the plant.

Next, build a thin, blue edge inside of the green square. This is the cell membrane which is made of a thin layer of fat and protein. It also surrounds the cell. The function of the cell's membrane is to let some substances pass through into the cell and block others from entering.

There are two large areas inside of the cell membrane—the nucleus and the vacuole.

Construct a somewhat circular area of bricks (we chose red for this) inside the cell membrane to create your nucleus. The nucleus is the control center of the cell and has many functions. The vacuole is a large space within a plant cell that is filled with fluid and helps the cell to keep its shape. To build the cell's vacuole, use white bricks to create a large shape on the baseplate.

Plant cells also have parts called the rough endoplasmic reticulum and smooth

endoplasmic reticulum (also referred to as Rough ER and Smooth ER). These sections are made up of folded sacs and tunnels; they transport materials through the cell.

Rough ER is located next to the nucleus, smooth ER buds off the rough ER. Use the brown bricks to build a section of rough ER next to the nucleus and the black bricks to construct an area of smooth ER beyond the rough ER.

Rough ER is covered with ribosomes, which are round structures that produce proteins. Use five of the 1x1 gray bricks to build ribosomes on the rough ER.

Next, build the nucleolus, a small organelle located within the nucleus, using cream colored bricks. This is where RNA is produced. There is also a single, round orange brick; this is the centrosome where microtubules are created. Microtubules provide structure and shape to plant cells.

Black bricks = Smooth ER
Brown bricks = Rough ER
Gray bricks = Ribosomes
Cream bricks = Nucleolus
Orange brick = Centrosome

The large open area to the left side of the nucleus and vacuole also hosts several cell parts. The large, red brick represents the cell's mitochondrion, where energy is converted for the cell to use. The cell's Golgi body (purple bricks) prepares protein and fat molecules for use by the cell. Single green bricks represent the cell's chloroplast, where chlorophyll is stored. The small, red brick is the cell's amyloplast. Its job is to make starch for the plant to use.

Single large red brick = Mitochondrion
Purple bricks = Golgi body
Single green bricks = Chloroplasts
Single gray bricks = Ribosomes
Small red brick = Amyloplast

Here is a look at a complete plant cell built from bricks!

BE A SCIENTIST: EXPLORE MORE!

Plant cells and animal cells have some similarities and differences. Research the different parts of an animal cell and see if you can build one with bricks!

EXPLORING THE SCIENCE OF TASTE

Have you ever wondered why certain foods taste sweet and others taste salty? The answer to that question is on the tip of your tongue! To better understand how our taste buds work, we are going to build a model of the human tongue and taste a few of your favorite foods.

BUILDING A MODEL OF THE HUMAN TONGUE

Humans have small sensory organs on their tongue called taste buds. Many of us have an average of ten thousand taste buds in our mouth that help us to distinguish foods that are sweet, salty, bitter, and sour. If you stick out your tongue and look in a mirror, you will see small bumps—those are called papillae and most of them include your taste buds!

For this project, you will need the following items:

- Thirty-five Red bricks of various sizes
- Four 2x3 and four 1x3 green bricks
- Four 2x4 and two 2x3 blue bricks
- Four 2x4 and four 2x3 yellow bricks
- Two 2x4 white or gray bricks
- A baseplate

SCIENCE VOCABULARY

PAPILLAE: sensory organs located on the surface of the human tongue, also called taste buds

You will also need a food from each category for tasting! Here are a few sample foods to try:

- **Sour:** lemon, pickles, yogurt
- **Sweet:** candy, maple syrup
- **Salty:** pretzels, snack chips
- **Bitter:** broccoli, grapefruit, cranberries, coffee, baking cocoa (without sugar in it)

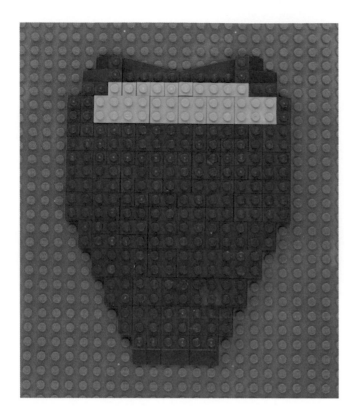

Begin this project by using red bricks to construct the shape of a tongue on your baseplate. The human tongue has a shape like a heart, wider at the top with a narrow bottom. The wider area of the tongue is located near the back of the mouth and the narrower section is the front part of the tongue.

Use the photo as a guide for building your brick tongue or find a mirror and look at your tongue before starting your build. Once the red area of the tongue is built, it is time to add the various taste buds to the model.

The first set of papillae will represent the area of the tongue that identifies foods with a bitter taste. Use green bricks to build a long, thin area across the top of your model. The taste buds across the back of your tongue are used when you eat foods such as grapefruit or broccoli.

Next, use yellow bricks to build two rectangular areas on the outside edges of your model below your green bricks. The yellow bricks represent papillae that help us to taste sour foods. These are the taste buds that activate when a person eats lemons, pickles, and yogurt.

The third set of taste buds are located closer to the front of the tongue and are used when we eat salty foods. Add blue bricks on the edges of your tongue model below the yellow bricks. This part of your tongue is used a lot if you enjoy eating pretzels, chips, and other salty snacks.

Have you noticed that we are only adding bricks to the outer edges of the tongue? The middle area of the tongue doesn't have many taste buds so it's the outer sides of your tongue that do all the work to help you identify the foods you are eating!

 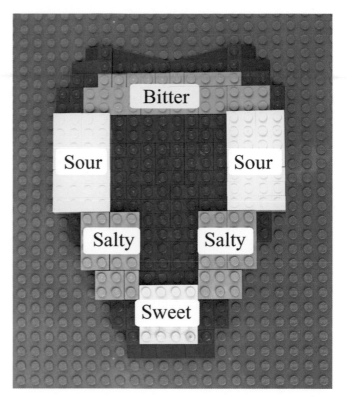

The last set of papillae are located right near the front tip of your tongue. Use the gray bricks to build the taste buds that are used when we eat sweet items such as candy, ice cream, and maple syrup.

BE A SCIENTIST: EXPLORE MORE!

Test your real tongue! Now that you know more about taste buds, eat a few of your favorite food items and try to feel which taste buds are stimulated while you chew.

Ask your family members to also try the same foods. Taste buds are different for each person and change as we age. You may enjoy eating cotton candy as a kid (which is very sweet) but adults may not like its super sweet taste. Adults prefer to drink coffee (which has a bitter taste) while children and teenagers usually shy away from bitter foods.

Brick Physics

Physics is the study of matter, energy, forces, and motion. This area of science helps us understand how the world works. Scientists who work in this branch of science are called physicists. The topics we will cover in this area include waves, sound, light, and motion.

The following experiments and projects will focus on physics concepts. First, we will explore the science of light and sound waves with the following brick projects:

- **Spell That Again? The Science of Reflection**
- **Water Refraction: Science Experiment or Magic Trick?**
- **Brick Shadows: Experimenting with Light**
- **Can You Hear Me? Brick Megaphone**

Then we will learn about forces such as gravity and buoyancy by doing some hands-on experiments:

- **Testing Speed Using Ramps & Brick Cars**
- **Weighing Objects with a Balance Scale**
- **Exploring How to Defy Gravity with Centripetal Force**
- **Creating a Balloon Launcher to Make Bricks Fly**
- **Testing Buoyancy by Answering the Question: Do Bricks Sink or Float?**

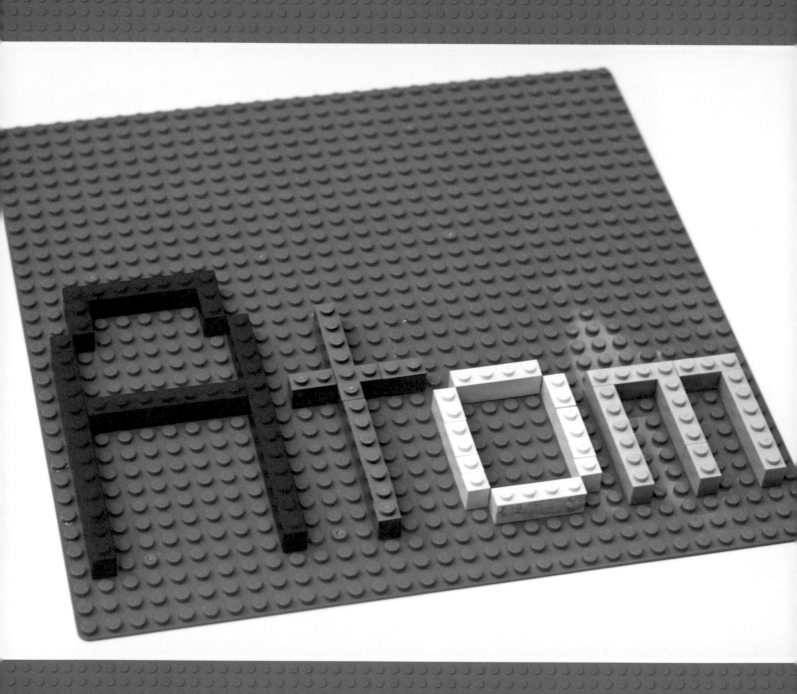

SPELL THAT AGAIN? THE SCIENCE OF REFLECTION

Did you know that mirrors can play tricks on you? When you look into a mirror, you are seeing a reflection of yourself or of the items you are holding up to the mirror.

To test this theory, we are going to do a brick science experiment with mirrors!

TESTING THE SCIENCE OF REFLECTION

For this experiment, you will need the following supplies:

- A mirror
- A baseplate
- Enough bricks to spell out your name (we used approximately forty bricks)

SCIENCE VOCABULARY

REFLECTION: an image produced by a mirror

PALINDROME: a word or phrase that reads the same way forward and backwards

PHOTONS: basic units that make up light

First, use the bricks to spell your first or last name on the baseplate. You can use a nickname if your real name has too many letters to fit on a baseplate. Or you can spell out the name of your pet if you would like to use a different name for the experiment.

Almost any name will do with one exception—if the letters in your name spell the same word both forwards and backwards, then you cannot use it for this experiment because your name is a *palindrome*.

A palindrome is any word, phrase, or sequence of letters that reads the same backward as forward. For example, the name Anna is a palindrome—if we reverse the letters, the word is still spelled the same: a-n-n-A.

Other common names that are palindromes include:

- **Ava**
- **Otto**
- **Elle**
- **Hannah**

The word "racecar" is also a palindrome—reverse the letters and it still spells out r-a-c-e-c-a-r!

A fun fact you can impress your friends and family with this week!

Sure, why not—we will use Atom's name for our experiment!

When you read the name on the baseplate, your eyes are scanning from left to right as they see the letters. Hold the baseplate up to a mirror. What do you see when you read the letters in order from left to right?

Here is what we see:

In the mirror, the letters now read m-o-t-A. The name on our baseplate is reversed so Atom's name becomes Mota! This is due to the mirror's reflective properties.

THE SCIENCE OF MIRRORS

A mirror has a smooth surface that reflects light. When rays of light (also called photons) hit a mirror's surface, they bounce back at the same angle and cause your eyes to see a reversed image. Most of the

mirrors we have in our homes and schools are flat, made of glass, and accurately reflect the objects in front of them.

We are taught to read words from left to right, but what happens if you try to read the name on your baseplate from right to left in the mirror? It is easy to read when doing it in this direction since we are reading a reflection of the word!

BE A SCIENTIST: EXPLORE MORE!

Repeat this experiment using a page from a book. Hold the open book up to a mirror. Are you able to read the words that are reflected back to you?

WATER REFRACTION: SCIENCE EXPERIMENT OR MAGIC TRICK?

During our last experiment, we learned how light waves reflect off a mirror's surface. This experiment will explore what happens to light waves as they enter water and how the science of refraction can trick our eyes to seeing something that is not really there!

SETTING UP THE EXPERIMENT

To complete this experiment, you will need the following items:

- A jar or glass filled with water
- A colored baseplate (the baseplate can NOT be the same color as the other bricks you use)
- Four 2x2 black bricks
- Two colored bricks (we used purple) with slanted sides (such as bricks that would be used to build a roof) or smaller bricks that can be shaped to create the pointed end of an arrow

Using the bricks, build an arrow in the center of your baseplate. Use the black bricks for the straight side of the arrow and the colored bricks to build the arrow's pointed end.

Once you have built the arrow, stand the baseplate up to the right side of the glass or jar of water with the arrow pointing toward the left.

THE SCIENCE OF REFRACTION

For this experiment to work correctly, you will need to look through the jar of water as the arrow passes behind it. Slowly, move your baseplate to the left, sliding it behind the water jar.

As the arrow reaches the jar of water, you should see the tail side of the arrow (the black bricks) on the right side of the jar while the colored point of the arrow will appear on the left side of the jar! It will look as though the arrow is broken and showing on both sides of your glass jar.

Continue to slide your baseplate to the left so the entire brick arrow is behind the water. Now what do you see? Our arrow appears to be pointing to the right now instead of pointing to the left—how did that happen?

If you continue to slide the baseplate to the left, the pointed edge of your arrow appears on the baseplate behind the jar while the straight edge is still behind the water. The colored edge of the arrow is pointing to the left even though it had just appeared to be pointing to the right.

HOW DOES WATER REFRACTION WORK?

Refraction is a concept that refers to the way a light wave travels through any medium such as water or glass. Light waves travel in a straight line through air; however, as light waves enter glass or water, they bend. The light waves are refracted as they pass through the glass and water.

As light travels into the glass of water, the waves bend toward the center. As the light continues through the glass and water, the light that was on the right side now appears on the left and the light that was on the left side now appears on the right. This shift causes the image of the brick arrow to be reversed. The brick arrow never changes directions. The glass of water is creating an optical illusion for our eyes.

BE A SCIENTIST: EXPLORE MORE!

What happens if you make a brick arrow on your baseplate that points up instead of to the side—does the newly built arrow reverse when you slide it behind the jar of water?

BRICK SHADOWS: EXPERIMENTING WITH LIGHT

If you have ever stood outside on a sunny day, you will notice that your body casts a shadow on the ground. Shadows occur when a solid object blocks a light source from shining through it. Not only will we create a shadow during this experiment, but we will also explore how shadows change over time.

SETTING UP THE EXPERIMENT

A clear, transparent object will not cast a shadow—light will just pass through it. So it is important to use solid bricks for this experiment!

Gather the following items for the experiment:

- A variety of solid bricks to build a structure
- Two pieces of light-colored paper
- A few pieces of tape
- A pencil or pen
- An outdoor location that receives at least three hours of sunlight

This experiment is best done outdoors during the afternoon hours. Try to begin the experiment around 1 p.m. for the best results.

SCIENCE VOCABULARY

SHADOW: a dark area that is produced when light is blocked by an opaque object

OPAQUE: a non-transparent object; something solid that you cannot see through

TRANSPARENT: a material that allows light to pass through it

PREDICTION: a forecast of what will happen based on observation or scientific reasoning

EXPLORING THE SCIENCE OF SHADOWS

Now we will measure the height of the shadow. Using the pencil or pen, draw a line at the top of the shadow and record the time of day next to the line. We began our experiment at 1:05 p.m.

Use your bricks to build a structure that measures at least seven bricks high and three bricks wide. Tall structures work better than wider structures for this experiment. For example, we built a thin tower that is fourteen bricks high and four bricks wide. The tower has a few openings where sunlight will shine through. Be creative with your structure!

Once you have a brick tower or structure built, tape the two shorter sides of light-colored paper together to create one long sheet. Then lay them on a flat surface outside in a sunny area. Place your brick structure on one edge of the paper. You should already see a shadow forming on the paper. If your shadow is not fully showing on the paper, turn your paper until you see a full shadow down the center of your paper.

After you mark the top of the shadow, make a prediction about how long the shadow will be after two hours have passed. Draw a second line to show the "estimated height" of the shadow. As you can see in the photo, we drew a line marked "estimated height" for our prediction of where the top of the shadow would fall at 3:05 pm. Leave the structure set up in the same location for the next two hours.

After two hours, check your shadow. How close is the top of your shadow to your prediction? When we checked our shadow at 3:10 p.m., it was quite a bit taller than our estimated height mark!

Remember, during the afternoon hours in the Northern Hemisphere, the sun is at its highest point at twelve noon. Less light is blocked by objects when the sun is directly overhead in the sky. As the day progresses, shadows grow longer as the sun continues to set towards the horizon.

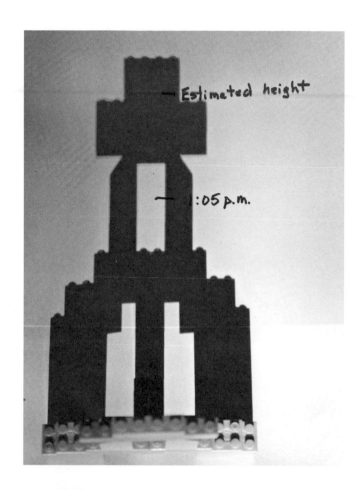

BE A SCIENTIST: EXPLORE MORE!

Begin your experiment at 8 a.m. instead of 12 noon. What do you notice about the shadows created from your structure at 8 a.m. versus the shadows you see at 12 noon? Why do you think this is?

FAST MOVING BRICKS: RAMPS & SPEED

Did you ever wonder why a bike or car moves faster when it is going downhill? Or maybe you have tried lying on the grass and rolling downhill (if you have not tried this, it is a lot of fun!). For this experiment, we will use a brick car and ramps to explore the force of gravity.

EXPERIMENTING WITH RAMPS

Gather the following items:

- A brick car (you can build one or use a pre-built brick vehicle)
- A flat board between twenty-four inches and forty inches long (to use as a ramp)
- A stopwatch or timer that records seconds
- Pencil and paper for recording time

SCIENCE VOCABULARY

GRAVITY: an invisible force that pulls items toward the Earth. Gravity also exists in space; it is the force that keeps the moon in orbit around the Earth.
RAMP: a flat surface with one end that is higher than the other
SPEED: how fast an object travels over a given area
INCLINE: a surface that has an angle and is higher on one side and lower on the other

For this experiment, we will use the flat board to create two different height ramps. The first will be a low ramp with a shallow incline. The second ramp will have a steeper incline than the first.

This photo shows how the board should be placed at different angles during the experiment. Our board is thirty-eight inches long. For the first part of the experiment, prop your board on an object that is approximately six to nine inches high. We used an empty plastic container to hold our board in place.

For the second part of the experiment, the board should be placed at a steeper angle. Prop your board on an item that is twelve to eighteen inches high. We placed our board on the seat of a chair. For the best results, your second ramp should be twice as high as your first.

Place your brick car at the top of your lower ramp. Get your stopwatch or timer ready! It would be a good idea if someone else recorded the time while you start the car down the ramp.

Release your car and start the timer! Stop the timer when your car reaches the bottom of the ramp. Record the car's time. Our car took 6.2 seconds to reach the bottom of our ramp. Now adjust your ramp's height so that it is twice as high as your original ramp. Then follow the same procedures again:

- **Release your car and start the timer!**
- **Stop the timer when your car reaches the bottom of the ramp**
- **Record the car's time**

Our brick car reached the bottom of our steeper ramp in 5.6 seconds!

Compare the speed of your car—which ramp produced the faster speed? For us, the higher ramp with the steeper slope allowed the car to travel faster to the bottom. Since the flat board and car were both the same, we can conclude that the steeper the ramp, the faster the car will travel.

BE A SCIENTIST: EXPLORE MORE!

Test your ramp using other items such as a marble or golf ball. Do these items also reach the bottom faster if the ramp has a steeper incline?

CAN YOU HEAR ME? BUILDING A BRICK MEGAPHONE

Have you ever wanted to make your voice louder without having to scream? Maybe someone asks, *"Who wants a cookie?"* and you want them to hear you say, *"I do!"* from the back of the room. For this project, we are going to build a brick megaphone and explore the science of sound waves.

BUILDING A MEGAPHONE

This is a creative build so use any color bricks you would like to create your megaphone. The only items you need for this project are bricks and your voice! Gather a variety of bricks that are 2x2, 2x3, 2x4, and 2x6. If you plan to include a handle, use 2x4 and 2x8 bricks.

SCIENCE VOCABULARY

SOUND WAVES: sound is created from vibrations; these vibrations form waves that move through solids, liquids (such as water), and gases (such as air)

MEGAPHONE: a funnel-shaped item that amplifies the voice

AMPLIFY: to increase the volume of a sound

Brick megaphones are built in layers like a pyramid except that a megaphone will have an opening at both the top and the bottom. To construct a megaphone, begin by laying bricks out on a table in a square or rectangular format. The bricks should be touching but not connected. As you begin to build the second layer, allow only the outer set of studs to show. Use the photo above as a guide.

Our first layer included green bricks and the second layer is blue bricks. Notice that as we build with the blue bricks, we only use the inside set of studs from the green bricks. This will result in a pyramid-shaped structure.

After our third layer of bricks, we added a handle to the bottom of our megaphone using some 1x4 and 2x8 bricks. Once the handle was in place, we continued to build layers using only the inside set of studs until we reached a point where only a small opening remained at the top.

This photo shows the completed megaphone from underneath.

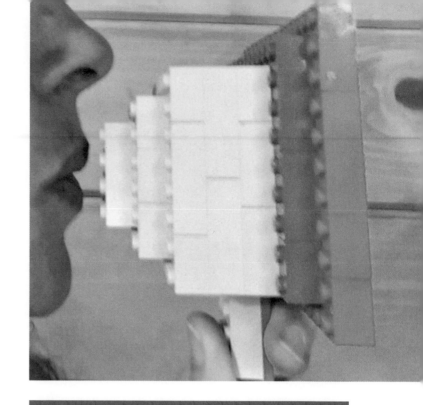

UNDERSTANDING THE SCIENCE OF SOUND WAVES

To use the brick megaphone, place the narrow side near your mouth and speak into it.

Megaphones work in two different ways. First, they funnel the sound waves coming out of your mouth into one direction. When you speak without a megaphone, sound waves leave your mouth and scatter in all directions—up, down, left, right and straight ahead. A megaphone collects those sound waves and sends them in the same direction.

The second way megaphones work is they help to amplify your voice by reflecting some of the sound waves as they travel down the funnel. As you speak, sound waves will enter the narrow side of the megaphone. The waves travel down the length of the megaphone to the wider end. Some of those sound waves bounce off the sides of the megaphone before they exit. This allows your voice to be amplified, which makes it sound louder.

BE A SCIENTIST: EXPLORE MORE!

Continue to build more brick layers on the bottom of the megaphone to make it longer. How does this impact the sound waves when you speak into it? Does your voice appear to be softer or louder with a longer megaphone?

WEIGHING OBJECTS WITH A BALANCE SCALE

Sometimes scientists need to know the mass of an object or whether one object is heavier than another. For example, how many pennies are equal to the weight of two quarters? A balance scale is a science tool that allows you to compare the weight of two objects or groups of items.

BUILDING A BALANCE SCALE

A balance scale looks a little like a teeter totter. It's an instrument that allows you to put items on both sides of the scale until the scale is no longer tilting to one side but instead becomes level, showing that the items on both sides have an equal amount of mass.

What is mass? Mass is commonly measured by how much something weighs in grams, kilograms, ounces, or pounds, but weight can change while mass stays the same. For example, the weight of an object on Earth is different from the

weight of an object on the moon but its mass is the same.

To build a balance scale, you will need the following items:

- One set of brick wheels
- One flat 2 x 16 brick
- Two flat 2 x 6 bricks
- Two flat 2 x 4 bricks
- Two 1 x 2 bricks

Attach the wheels to the center of your 2 x 16 brick. Then add your 2 x 6 bricks to the top of each side of the 2 x 16 brick (we attached ours to the first two rows of studs.)

Next, add your 2 x 4 bricks to the top side of the 2 x 6 bricks, again using two studs. Finally, attach your 1 x 2 bricks to the outer studs of your 2 x 4 bricks. These serve as an edge to the sides of your scale so that items will not slide off.

Now it's time to use the scale!

MEASURING ITEMS ON A BALANCE SCALE

What can you put on the scale? We decided to compare the mass of various coins. For example, we learned that the mass of a nickel is approximately the same as the mass of two pennies.

Notice that both sides of the scale are almost level in the photo above—this indicates that the scale is "in balance" and the items on each side have a similar mass.

If one side of your scale is higher than the other, that means that one of your items has a greater mass than the other.

Here is the view of the scale from the top. Atom decided the scale looked like fun, so he pushed off the pennies and jumped on!

As you can see, Atom is way up in the air while the other side of the scale holding the nickel is touching the table. The two sides of the scale are out of balance! This tells us that Atom's mass is much less than the mass of the nickel.

BE A SCIENTIST: EXPLORE MORE!

Test your balance scale using items from around your home such as small rocks, erasers, paper clips, or small toys. Which has a larger mass — a small rock or three coins? Does a pencil eraser have a mass greater or less than three coins?

HOW TO DEFY GRAVITY: CENTRIPETAL FORCE

Have you ever tried to spin a lasso over your head? Or ridden on an upside-down roller coaster? What keeps the lasso in the air or you from falling off the ride? Our next experiment is going to explore how centripetal force works to keep things spinning instead of falling to the ground.

SETTING UP THE EXPERIMENT

Collect the following items for this experiment:

- A four-foot piece of string or twine
- A plastic cup
- A hole punch or sharp pencil
- A brick minifigure

This experiment will show us how Newton's First Law of Motion works. Isaac Newton was a famous scientist who worked with the forces found in nature. Newton's First Law of Motion tells us that an object in motion will stay in motion at the same speed and direction unless acted on by another force.

SCIENCE VOCABULARY

CENTRIPETAL FORCE: a force that keeps an object moving in a circular path, pulling the object toward the center of the rotation

GRAVITY: a force that pulls an object toward the center of the Earth

FORCE: a push or pull that is exerted on an object

First, we need to use the cup and twine to build a holder for our brick minifigure. Use the hand-held hole punch to make four holes around the top edge of the plastic cup. If a hand-held hole punch is not available, you can also use a sharp pencil to create the holes (ask an adult to help with this step). Then thread the string or twine through the holes and tie a knot in the string over the center of the cup. Use the photo above as a guide for preparing the cup. Once completed, place your brick minifigure into the cup. Charlie volunteered to help with this experiment.

TESTING CENTRIPETAL FORCE

Now comes the fun part! To be able to see centripetal force in action, you will be swinging the cup in a full circle. Find a wide-open area either inside or outdoors. Be sure there is not anything above or behind you that the cup may hit once it begins to move.

Hold the top of the string in your hand and extend your arm straight out to your side. The cup should dangle right below your hand.

Begin to slowly swing the cup back and forth like a pendulum. If you watch, the cup is beginning to swing along a circular pathway. While swinging the cup back and forth, you are building up the force that is needed to keep your brick minifigure from falling out. As the cup reaches a point where it is almost parallel to the ground, swing it harder so the cup makes a complete circle.

Continue swinging the cup in a full circle at least four or five times. You should be able to feel that force in the string you are holding. Even though the cup is very light, you will feel a pull on the string as the cup begins to make a circular motion. The pull that you feel is the cup wanting to move in a straight line; however, your swinging of the string is pulling the cup in a circle.

As the cup swings higher, the minifigure is pushed to the bottom of the cup. When the cup is fully upside down, two things could happen. One is that centripetal force is strong enough to keep the minifigure inside the cup. The second is that the force of gravity is stronger and pulls the minifigure to the ground. If your minifigure falls out of the cup as it spins, place it back inside and try spinning your cup faster.

Once the cup has spun around in four or five full circles, slow down the spinning until the cup is resting below your hand in the same position you started. Is your brick minifigure still inside the cup?

BE A SCIENTIST: EXPLORE MORE!

What happens if you put more than one brick minifigure in the cup? Add a few more bricks to your cup and repeat the experiment. Do you have to spin the cup faster for all the bricks to remain inside?

CAN YOU MAKE YOUR BRICKS FLY? BALLOON LAUNCHER

One of our brick scientists, Atom, has always wondered what it would feel like to fly. But like all of us on Earth, gravity is holding him in place. At first, Atom thought he might make himself a set of wings to see if he could fly like a bird. Instead, we thought we would help him out with this fun science project—creating a balloon launcher that will propel Atom into the air.

BUILDING A BALLOON LAUNCHER

For this experiment, you will need the following items:

- A plastic cup
- A balloon
- A pair of scissors
- Tape
- A brick minifigure

SCIENCE VOCABULARY

FORCE: a push or pull that is exerted on an object; force has both magnitude and direction

MOTION: an object's change in position

SPEED: how fast an object moves over a given area

To prepare the balloon launcher, use scissors to carefully cut off the bottom of the plastic cup. Then wrap tape around the cut edge of the cup so all sharp edges are covered. Next, tie a knot in the uninflated balloon. Carefully cut a small section (approximately one-half an inch) off the top of the balloon so there is a small hole. Stretch the balloon around the uncut edge of the cup so the knot is in the center of the cup facing outward. The knotted end of the balloon will be pulled down during the experiment.

Test your launcher by slowly pulling the knot down and away from the cup. The balloon should stretch away from but not fall off the cup.

Insert the brick minifigure into the cup. When you look down into your launcher, you should see both the minifigure and the inside part of the knot on the balloon.

TESTING THE BALLOON LAUNCHER

Now find a large open area to test your launcher. We recommend doing this experiment outdoors to allow for enough room that the minifigure does not hit a ceiling or light fixture.

Once outside, hold the bottom of the launcher (the side covered with the balloon) in one hand. Be sure to point the launcher away from you and any other people or pets. Be sure the open end of the cup is pointing upward toward the sky. With your other hand, carefully pull down on the knot and then quickly release it. Your minifigure should fly into the air!

Remember Newton's First Law of Motion from our last experiment? When an object is not moving, Newton's First Law of Motion tells us that an object at rest will stay at rest unless it is acted on by a force. When we put the brick minifigure into our balloon launcher, it is "an object at rest." Nothing will happen to it unless a force is created. By pulling down on the knot and releasing it, we are creating a force.

The amount of force behind an object will affect both the distance the object moves and the speed of the object. As a force increases, speed and distance also increase. What happens if you pull the knot down farther before releasing it? Does your minifigure fly higher into the air?

BE A SCIENTIST: EXPLORE MORE!

Hold the cup so the opening is pointing sideways instead of facing upward. Be sure the cup is not pointing toward any person or pets. Now pull the knot to launch your minifigure. Does it still fly as high as when the cup was pointing upward?

TESTING BUOYANCY: DO BRICKS SINK OR FLOAT?

Have you ever played with your bricks in water? Maybe you took them into the bathtub to build a boat or submarine? This experiment is going to test whether bricks will sink or float in water (caution: you might get a little wet).

PREPARING THE EXPERIMENT

The following supplies are needed for this experiment:

- A jar or cup
- Some water
- A brick minifigure
- A piece of paper and a pencil

Before we begin the experiment, there are a few things to discuss. The first is a force called buoyancy. Buoyancy is an upward force that helps support an item while it is in water. If you have ever tried to float on your back in water, this is the force that helps keep you from sinking. Buoyancy is the reason we feel lighter when we are in a pool, lake, or ocean.

Another factor that will influence our experiment is density. All items are made

SCIENCE VOCABULARY

DENSITY: the mass of an item in relation to its volume
BUOYANCY: an upward force that supports an item in water
PREDICTION: a forecast of what will happen based on observation or scientific reasoning.

up of molecules. The closer together those molecules are, the denser the item. The density of an item gives us a clue as to whether the item will sink or float. An item does not need to weigh a lot to sink. For example, both a small rock and a very large rock will sink when they are placed in a jar of water. This is because both rocks are more dense than the water.

For this experiment, our prediction is that bricks are less dense than water, thus they will float. We are going to put Charlie in water to test our prediction that bricks will float instead of sink.

"Don't worry Charlie, I am pretty sure you won't have to swim."

This is the easiest experiment in the whole book! First, fill the jar or cup halfway with water. Next, make a prediction about what you think will happen. You may be using a different type of minifigure than we are using for our experiment. When you place your brick minifigure in the cup of water, what do you think will happen? Write your prediction down on a piece of paper.

Ok Charlie, time to get wet!

"Hey, Charlie . . ."
I really don't like the water! What if there are sharks?!
"Charlie, you are floating on the water. And sharks only swim in the ocean, not in a jar!"

Did your minifigure float or sink? Was your prediction correct?

BE A SCIENTIST: EXPLORE MORE!

Volume is how much space something takes up—so an adult has a greater volume than a child since the adult takes up more space. Test a sink and float prediction if you stack a set of bricks (more volume) together and put them in water versus if you just place one brick in the jar of water. Does the stack of bricks still float?

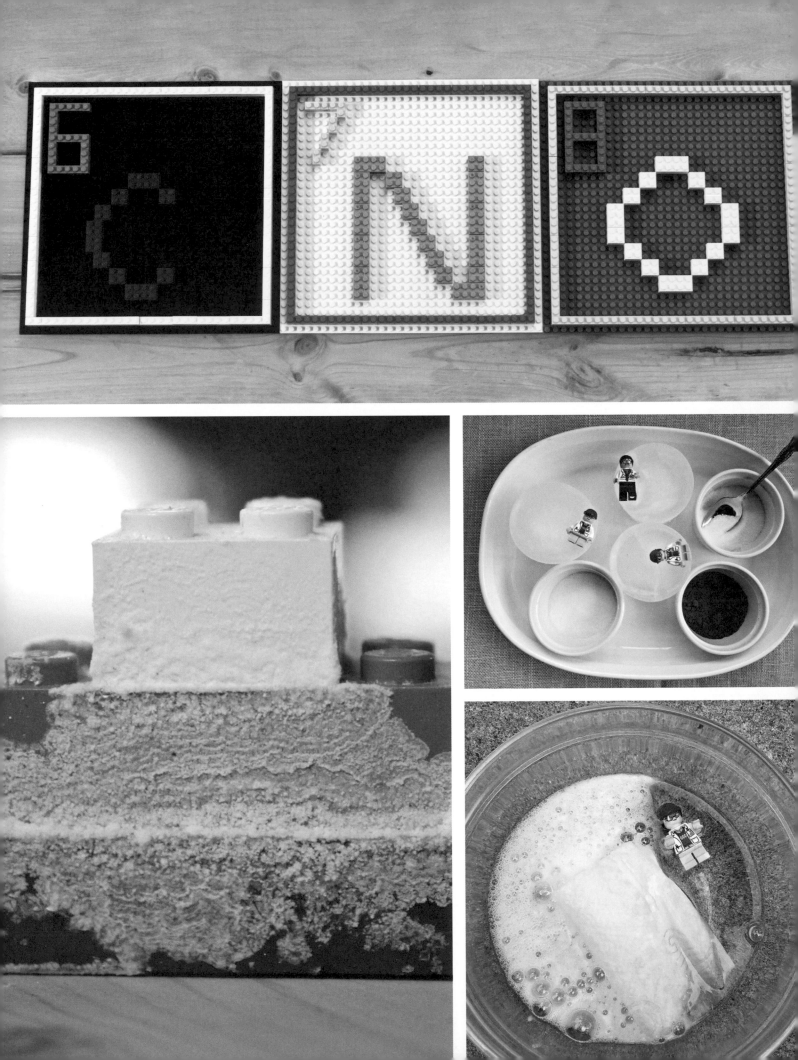

Brick Chemistry

Chemistry is the study of substances that make up matter, and matter is everything in the universe. It is the branch of science that focuses on atoms, elements, compounds, and mixtures. People who work in this area of science are called chemists.

As we explore chemistry, we will use bricks for the following experiments and projects:

- Understanding Buoyancy in Salt Water versus Fresh Water
- Growing Salt Crystals on Bricks
- Experimenting with Water and Pepper to Understand Surface Tension
- Testing Substances that Can Melt Ice to Rescue Brick Minifigures
- Using a Chemical Mixture to Make a Brick Scientist Disappear
- Creating an Invisible Gas
- Building a Model of the Periodic Table

WHAT'S IN THE WATER? SALT WATER VS. FRESH WATER

In our last experiment, we tested whether bricks sink or float (and lucky for Charlie, we learned he could float!). For this experiment, we are going to find out if bricks will sink or float in different types of water! Again, you may get a little wet with this activity so remember to roll up your sleeves and put down a towel before you begin.

TESTING BUOYANCY IN FRESH WATER

Collect the following items for this experiment:

- A large bowl
- One cup of table salt
- Three cups of water
- A brick minifigure
- A large brick with an open side that will act as a raft for your minifigure

Charlie is going to help again with this water experiment. Remember, Charlie does not like water (and he is afraid of sharks), so he does not want to sink.

SCIENCE VOCABULARY

DENSITY: the mass of an item in relation to its volume

BUOYANCY: an upward force that supports an item in water

SALINITY: the amount of salt dissolved in a body of water

TRANSPARENT: a material that allows light to pass through it; something you can see through

OPAQUE: a non-transparent object; something solid that you are not able to see through

Fill a bowl with three cups of water. Next, lay your large brick on the water and place your minifigure inside the hollow area of the brick. As you can see in the photo, both the hollow brick and Charlie float on the top of the water. Now it is time to test to see how many coins it will take to sink the brick raft.

No one told me the raft would sink!!

"*Don't worry Charlie! Remember the last experiment; you float in water. And I have already checked the bowl—there are no sharks!*"

First, place one coin in the brick raft. We used a penny. The raft is still floating with Charlie and one penny on it. Keep adding coins one by one until your brick raft sinks.

If you do not have any coins, you can also add other small items such as paperclips or marbles.

Our brick raft sunk to the bottom of the bowl after we added three coins to it. And Charlie was still floating on the water even without a raft.

TESTING BUOYANCY IN SALTWATER

Now that we know how many coins the raft will hold in fresh water, we are going to change the salinity of the water by adding salt to it. Ocean water has a higher level of salinity than fresh water too. Our prediction is that objects in salt water are more buoyant than objects in fresh water, so the raft should be able to hold more weight.

Remove the raft, coins, and minifigure from your bowl of water. Then, carefully pour in one cup of salt and stir the water. The first thing you may notice is that the water in your bowl is no longer transparent. The salt will make it very cloudy and opaque, so it is harder to see through it.

Once the salt is mixed into the water, place your brick raft and minifigure back in the bowl so they are floating on the water. Now, repeat the same steps from the first part of the experiment, adding one coin at a time to the brick raft to see how many coins it will hold before it sinks.

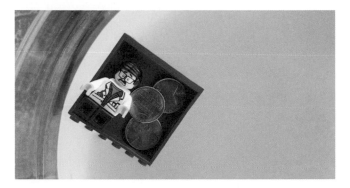

Will you look at that! There are three coins in the raft with Charlie and it is still floating!

Remember the first part of the experiment? Once we added a third coin, the raft sank to the bottom of the bowl. This tells us that heavier objects are more buoyant in salt water than in fresh water.

"Hey Charlie, what do you think will happen when we put the fourth coin on the raft?"

Umm... I hope it stays afloat!

Let's see if Charlie is right!

"Oh no! Sorry, Charlie. That fourth coin made the raft sink."

So, what did we learn—other than the fact that Charlie does not like to get wet? First, we learned that weight decreases buoyancy. As we added more weight to the raft, it became less buoyant, eventually sinking. We also learned that a heavy object is more likely to stay afloat in salt water than in fresh water. This is due to the density of the water; salt water is denser than fresh water.

BE A SCIENTIST: EXPLORE MORE!

Try repeating this experiment using other liquids such as apple juice or milk. Can you find a liquid that is more dense than salt water?

BRICK CAMOUFLAGE: GROWING SALT CRYSTALS

Did you know that you can change the color of your bricks? Yep, we are going to show you how to turn your red and blue bricks into white ones with this quick science experiment using salt.

PREPARING THE EXPERIMENT

This experiment requires the following supplies:

- Table salt (also called iodized salt)
- A pot
- An adult to help you use the stove
- Two cups of boiling water
- A glass bowl
- One cup of table salt
- A small towel
- Six to ten red and/or blue bricks
- A heavy kitchen item or rock (something that can get wet and hold your bricks under water)

SCIENCE VOCABULARY

SALINITY: the amount of salt dissolved in a body of water

CRYSTALS: a solid material whose molecules or atoms are arranged in a regularly repeating pattern

ATOMS: the tiny building blocks that make up matter

MOLECULES: a group of atoms that bond together

First, build a small tower or pyramid with the red and blue bricks. The structure should only be three bricks high; short enough to be fully submerged in the water in your bowl.

An adult will need to help with the next part of this experiment since it requires the use of a stove or microwave. Heat two cups of water in a pot on the stovetop or in the microwave using a microwave-safe measuring up. Once the water is heated to boiling, add in one cup of salt and stir. Once it is mixed, pour the salt water in a glass bowl.

The water will look cloudy when you first add it to the bowl.

GROWING SALT CRYSTALS

Next, carefully place your brick structure in the water (you may need to use tongs to do this if the water is still hot) and weigh it down with the rock or another heavy item.

Leave your brick structure submerged in water for at least eight hours (leaving it overnight would be ideal!) After eight or more hours, carefully remove your brick structure. When you take it out of the bowl, do NOT wipe it off! Just place the brick structure on a plate or small towel in a dry place (for example, on a kitchen counter).

After six to eight hours, you will begin to see a white dust appear near the edges of the bricks (pretty cool!). The white areas you see on the bricks are salt crystals forming as the bricks dry.

Continue to leave the brick structure undisturbed on a counter for the next few days. As more time passes, the water on the bricks will continue to evaporate, leaving behind white salt crystals.

How do crystals form? The first thing you need to grow crystals is a super-saturated solution. When you mix a lot of salt into a small amount of water as we did, not all the salt is dissolved. As the heated water cools and then evaporates, the salt stays behind. The salt molecules gather in a repeating pattern on surfaces such as the bricks and bottom of the bowl, forming crystals.

BE A SCIENTIST: EXPLORE MORE!

Try the experiment again but this time add one cup of sugar to the water instead of salt. Are you able to grow crystals on your bricks using sugar?

DON'T MAKE ME SNEEZE! SURFACE TENSION EXPERIMENT

If you look outside after it has rained, you will see water beading up in droplets and small pools. Water molecules like to stick together giving water special properties. One of these properties is called surface tension. This experiment will explore how surface tension works!

Ada is going to help us with this experiment because she enjoys getting her feet wet. But Ada does not like to sneeze! We must be sure that we do not let Ada get too close to the black pepper we are using for the experiment.

SETTING UP THE EXPERIMENT

You will need the following items for this experiment:

- A small plate
- Water
- A small measuring cup
- Black pepper
- Dish soap
- A brick minifigure

SCIENCE VOCABULARY

HYDROPHOBIC: an object that will not mix with water

SURFACE TENSION: a property of a liquid that allows it to resist external forces

To prepare the experiment, pour a small amount of water onto the surface of the plate. It should be enough to cover the plate while not leaking over the sides. We used ¼ cup of water on our plate. Next, sprinkle black pepper over the water. The pepper will float on top of the water. This is because pepper is hydrophobic. Your plate should look like the photo above.

Now, rub dish soap onto the bottom of your minifigure. As you can see in the photo, we placed dish soap on Ada's feet.

WATCHING SURFACE TENSION IN ACTION

Time to get Ada's feet wet! Slowly, lower your minifigure onto the center of the plate.

As the minifigure's feet touch the water, you will see the black pepper quickly scatter to the edges of the plate or fall below the water's surface!

Why does this happen? Water has very high surface tension meaning the water molecules pull hard to stay close together. Dish soap breaks down the surface tension of water. This explains why soap is a good way to clean your hands and dishes! As the dish soap touches the water and breaks the tension, the water molecules work hard to stay together so they pull away from the soap and take the pepper with them.

BE A SCIENTIST: EXPLORE MORE!

Try this experiment with something other than dish soap. Try putting maple syrup or olive oil on the minifigure to see if the pepper moves away once it touches the water's surface.

RESCUE MISSION: HOW FAST DOES ICE MELT?

Have you ever dreamed about going on a rescue mission? We need your help! Our brick scientists are frozen in blocks of ice and we need to get them out fast. Help us figure out which items we can use to melt the ice as quickly as possible!

SETTING UP THE EXPERIMENT

Gather the following supplies for this activity:

- Three brick minifigures
- Three plastic cups
- Water
- Salt
- Sugar
- Cinnamon

SCIENCE VOCABULARY

IONIC COMPOUND: a compound formed by ions that bond together through electrostatic forces; table salt is an ionic compound

FREEZING POINT: the temperature at which liquid turns into a solid

To set up this experiment, fill each of the plastic cups halfway with water. Then place a brick minifigure in each cup. The minifigures will float on the top of the water. Next, put the cups into a freezer for a few hours until the water becomes ice.

When the cups are removed from the freezer, each of the brick minifigures will be attached to a frozen block of ice. It is our job to thaw them out as fast as possible!

EXPERIMENTING WITH FREEZING POINTS

Some substances will reduce the melting point of ice so that it thaws quicker. We have three items we can test to see if they help melt the ice: salt, sugar, and cinnamon. Sprinkle the salt over one of the minifigures, the sugar over the second figure, and the cinnamon over the third one.

Carefully watch the ice under each minifigure for the next sixty seconds to see if there are any changes. Do you notice any melting taking place?

After a minute or two have passed, try lifting your minifigures off of the ice. Begin with the figure you covered in sugar. We sprinkled sugar over Ada (she has a sweet tooth). But when we try to lift her off the ice, she is still stuck.

Next, we tried to remove Charlie from his ice block. We sprinkled Charlie with cinnamon (since both Charlie and cinnamon begin with the same letter). But Charlie is still frozen solid to his block of ice too!

Our last chance is to rescue Atom, who was covered with the salt. When we look at Atom's ice block, we can see some areas of water already forming. Could the salt be working?

When we lift Atom, he is no longer frozen to the ice!

So why were we able to save Atom from the ice block but both Charlie and Ada are still frozen in place? It was all due to the items we sprinkled on each block of ice. Fresh water freezes at 32°F or 0°C. Salt water has a freezing point of 28°F or -2° C. This means that the temperature needs to be colder to freeze salt water than fresh water.

When ice meets salt, the salt makes it difficult for the water molecules to bond together. This reaction causes the film on the top of ice to begin to melt and change to a liquid (water). Since Atom was frozen to the top of the ice block, once we placed salt on the ice, it lowered the freezing point and Atom was released. While sugar and cinnamon will both help to lower the

freezing point and melt ice, it will take longer for these substances to work than it will for salt. You can use a timer to record how long it will take for the cinnamon and sugar to melt the ice.

BE A SCIENTIST: EXPLORE MORE!

Repeat the experiment using three different types of salt such as table salt, rock salt, Epsom salt, or kosher salt. Does one type of salt work quicker than the others to melt the ice?

CAN YOU MAKE A BRICK SCIENTIST DISAPPEAR?

For this experiment, we are going to create a chemical reaction by combining a solid (baking soda) with a liquid (vinegar) to form a gas. In the process, we will also make one of our brick figures disappear!

PREPARING THE EXPERIMENT

The following items are needed for this experiment:

- A bowl
- A measuring cup
- A teaspoon
- One cup of white vinegar
- Two teaspoons of baking soda
- A paper towel
- A brick minifigure

SCIENCE VOCABULARY

CHEMICAL REACTION: the process where one or more substances are changed into a different substance

CO_2: carbon dioxide, a colorless and invisible gas

BAKING SODA: its scientific name is sodium bicarbonate; baking soda is a base

To prepare the experiment, fill a bowl with one cup of white vinegar. Next, measure out two teaspoons of baking soda and place it in the center of a paper towel. Then roll the paper towel into a long tube so the baking soda remains in the middle.

Place the brick minifigure into the bowl of vinegar. As you can see in the photo, vinegar is transparent, meaning you are able to see through the liquid. Next, place the folded paper towel on top of the vinegar in the bowl.

As the paper towel absorbs the vinegar, the baking soda will begin to leak out into the bowl. Mixing baking soda and vinegar will create a chemical reaction since one substance (baking soda) is a base and the other substance (vinegar) is an acid. This reaction will produce a lot of bubbles as it forms a gas called carbon dioxide.

As the reaction continues, more and more bubbles will form and rise to the top of the bowl! And before you know it . . .

. . . so many bubbles form that the brick minifigure will disappear!

BE A SCIENTIST: EXPLORE MORE!

Have you ever seen a volcano explode? This is another way you can experiment with a baking soda and vinegar reaction. Using clay or playdough, build a volcano-shaped mold around an empty plastic cup. Be sure to leave the top of the cup and volcano open. Once the volcano is completed, pour vinegar into the cup. Then add the folded paper towel with the baking soda to the cup and stand back! You should see the liquid expand quickly and the bubbles will rise to the top of your volcano making it look like an explosion.

WAKE UP ADA! HOW TO CREATE A GAS

Like all scientists, Ada works very hard and sometimes forgets to get a good night's sleep. She wants to take a quick nap today but needs to be sure she wakes up on time. To make sure she does not oversleep, we are going to create a chemical reaction that will wake her up!

Just like our last experiment with the disappearing scientist, this activity is also a chemical reaction. However, this time we will be able to SEE the gas (carbon dioxide) being produced when we mix baking soda with vinegar.

SCIENCE VOCABULARY

CHEMICAL REACTION: the process by which one or more substances are converted into a different substance

CO_2: carbon dioxide, a colorless and invisible gas

BAKING SODA: its scientific name is sodium bicarbonate; baking soda is a base

GAS: a substance that will expand freely and has no fixed shape and no fixed volume

SETTING UP THE EXPERIMENT

For this experiment, gather the following supplies:

- One plastic sandwich bag with a zip-lock seal
- One-quarter cup of white vinegar
- One paper towel
- Two teaspoons of baking soda
- A brick minifigure

Just like our last experiment, measure out two teaspoons of baking soda, place it in the center of a paper towel, and roll the paper towel into a long tube keeping the baking soda in the center. Unlike our last experiment, this one could get messy so we suggest doing the experiment outdoors or in a sink.

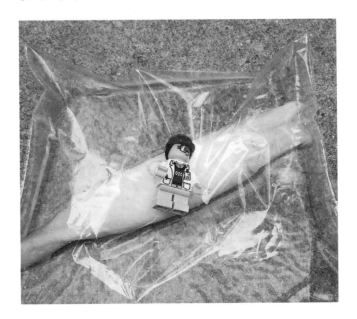

Pour one-quarter cup of vinegar into a zip-lock sandwich bag. Quickly place the paper towel with baking soda into the bag and seal the bag. Then lay your brick minifigure on the bag for a quick nap!

If enough carbon dioxide is produced during the experiment, your bag may explode since the expansion of the gas could be stronger than the seal on the bag. Be sure to step back after you seal the bag in case the seal pops open!

As the paper towel absorbs the vinegar in the bag, the baking soda will also mix with the vinegar. This creates a chemical reaction and produces the gas, carbon dioxide. As you can see in the photo, the bag is starting to get larger.

Since the bag is sealed, the gas cannot escape. Instead, the bag will start to inflate just like a balloon. As more carbon dioxide is made, the bag will fully inflate, sliding the brick minifigure onto their feet and waking them up!

BE A SCIENTIST: EXPLORE MORE!

Another fun way to try this experiment is by using a balloon attached to the top of a bottle. First, add the vinegar to a clean, empty bottle. Then place the baking soda inside a balloon (it does not need to be wrapped in a paper towel). Carefully expand the open side of the balloon to fit over the top of the bottle without releasing the baking soda. Once the balloon is covering the top of the bottle, shake the baking soda into the bottle. The reaction of vinegar and baking soda will create carbon dioxide gas which will inflate the balloon!

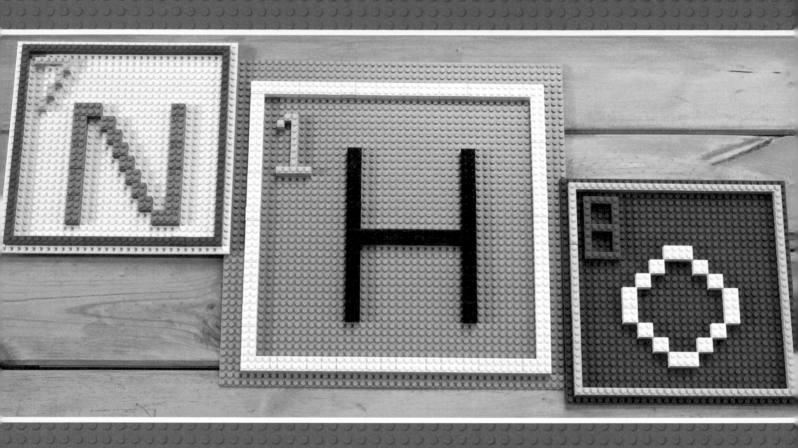

BRICK MODEL: ELEMENTS OF THE PERIODIC TABLE

Everything in the world is made up of elements or a combination of elements. An element is a substance that cannot be broken down into a simpler item. The periodic table is a picture of all the elements that exist on Earth. Each square on the periodic table shows the name of the element, its symbol, and the atomic number. There are currently 118 elements that exist on Earth; however, new elements are discovered every decade!

There are four main elements that make up ninety-six percent of the human body—carbon, oxygen, hydrogen, and nitrogen. For this science activity, we are going to build squares from the periodic table and learn more about each of these four elements!

SCIENCE VOCABULARY

ELEMENT: a substance that cannot be broken down into a simpler item

PERIODIC TABLE: a chart that lists all the elements in order by atomic number

ATOMIC NUMBER: the number of protons in the nucleus of an atom. This number determines where the element falls on the periodic table.

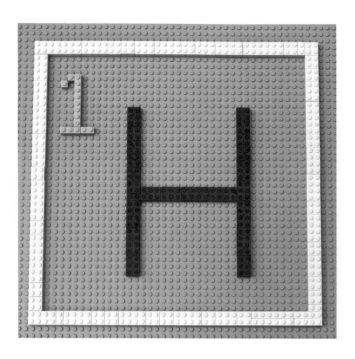
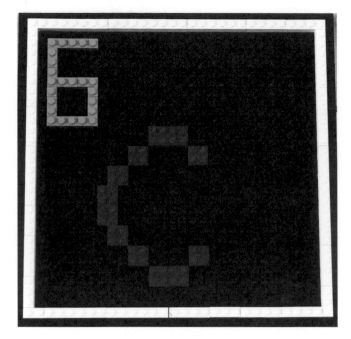

CONSTRUCTING SECTIONS OF THE PERIODIC TABLE

For this project, the following items are needed: one brick baseplate for each periodic square and bricks in three different colors.

For example, the first element on the periodic table is hydrogen. Its symbol is an "H" and its atomic number is 1.

To create an element square, build a square frame around the baseplate using one color of your bricks. Then use a second color of bricks to build an "H" in the center of the frame. Using the third color of bricks, create a number "1" in the upper left side of the frame. This is called the atomic number.

Hydrogen was recognized as an element in 1766, more than 250 years ago! Hydrogen is found in water. It is also found on the sun, stars, and the planet Jupiter.

Carbon is element number 6 on the periodic table with a symbol of "C." Carbon is found in the lead of pencils. When carbon bonds with oxygen, carbon dioxide is created. When humans exhale, we breathe out carbon dioxide. Create a periodic table square for carbon by building a "C" in the center of your baseplate and a number "6" in the upper left corner.

Two other popular elements include nitrogen and oxygen. Nitrogen has an atomic number of 7 and its symbol is an "N." Nitrogen is a colorless, odorless gas. It makes up seventy-eight percent of the air on Earth.

Element 8 on the periodic table is oxygen, which is one of the most well-known elements. When oxygen bonds with hydrogen, it makes water. Oxygen is also found in the air we breathe.

BE A SCIENTIST: EXPLORE MORE!

Research the element of iron and create a brick square with its element number and symbol. What do you notice about iron's symbol that is different from the other element squares we built?

Categories of Science Activities

BUILDING MODELS

Exploring the Parts of a Leaf

Constructing a Brick Plant Cell

Layers of the Atmosphere

The Water Cycle

The Science of Taste: Model of the Human Tongue

Create Your Own Brick Insect

Elements of the Periodic Table

Building Constellations

HANDS-ON EXPERIMENTS

Don't Make Me Sneeze! Surface Tension & Pepper

Spell That Again: The Science of Reflection

Brick Shadows: Experiment with Light

Rescue Mission: How Fast Does Ice Melt?

Do Bricks Sink or Float?

What's in the Water? Saltwater vs. Fresh Water

Water Refraction: Science Experiment or Magic Trick?

Can You Make Your Bricks Fly? Balloon Launcher

Brick Camouflage: Growing Salt Crystals

Fast Moving Bricks: Ramps & Speed

How to Defy Gravity: Centripetal Force

Can You Make a Brick Scientist Disappear?

Wake Up Ada! How to Create a Gas

SCIENCE TOOLS & PROJECTS

Recommended Project Learning Levels

Projects are grouped by learning level based on the scientific concepts used for each activity.

BEGINNER (AGES PRESCHOOL THROUGH SECOND GRADE)

> DIY Brick Dinosaur Dig
>
> Telling Time with a Brick Sundial
>
> Creating Your Own Brick Insect
>
> Designing a Bug Hotel
>
> Animal Armor: Engineering an Exoskeleton
>
> Exploring the Parts of a Leaf
>
> Building Constellations
>
> Brick Shadows: Experimenting with Light
>
> Fast Moving Bricks: Ramps & Speed
>
> Can You Make Your Bricks Fly? Balloon Launcher
>
> Testing Buoyancy: Do Bricks Sink or Float?
>
> Can You Make a Brick Scientist Disappear?
>
> Don't Make Me Sneeze! Surface Tension Experiment
>
> Rescue Mission: How Fast Does Ice Melt?

INTERMEDIATE (THIRD GRADE THROUGH FIFTH GRADE)

> Learning the Layers of the Atmosphere
>
> Creating a Model of the Water Cycle
>
> Making 2D and 3D Bar Graphs
>
> Brick Worm Viewer & Habitat

10 9 8 7 6 5 4 3 2

Library of Congress Cataloging-in-Publication Data is available on file.

Cover design by Brian Peterson
Cover and interior photography by Jacquie Fisher

Print ISBN: 978-1-5107-4966-5
E-Book ISBN: 978-1-5107-4967-2

Printed in China